MW00772349

Brewing Tea

Appreciating Chinese Tea

Written by Li Hong

Translated by Yilise Lin

CHINA INTERCONTINENTAL PRESS

WORLD CULTURE BOOKS

图书在版编目（CIP）数据

烹茶技艺：英文/李洪著；(新加坡)罗宇思(Yilise Lin)译.
-北京：五洲传播出版社，2009.12
ISBN 978-7-5085-1713-1

Ⅰ.①烹… Ⅱ.①李… ②罗… Ⅲ.①茶-文化-中国-英文 Ⅳ.①TS971

中国版本图书馆CIP数据核字（2009）第199693号

著　　者：李　洪
译　　者：Yilise Lin（新加坡）
选题编辑：荆孝敏 世界文化图书
责任编辑：王　莉 Lisa Zhang
装帧设计：宋索迪
设计制作：世界文化图书

出版发行：五洲传播出版社
地　　址：北京市海淀区北小马厂6号华天大厦
邮　　编：100038
网　　址：www.cicc.org.cn
电　　话：010-58891281
印　　刷：恒美印务（广州）有限公司
开　　本：889×1194mm　1 / 32
印　　张：5
版　　次：2010年1月第1版 2010年1月第1次印刷
07980（平）

Contents

Tea Set Suppliers: Li Hong,
Wang Jidong, Li Mei

Creative Director: Li Mei

Thanks to Jing Xiaomin, Li Mei, Madhumita Bardhan Sinha, Wang Li, Lisa Zhang and Suodi Song for their tireless efforts to make the project possible.

The Art of Brewing Tea

The purpose of learning the art of brewing tea is not to master the exact steps and actions of a professional teahouse server. Drinking tea is synonymous to relaxation. Focusing on the minutiae instead of enjoying the process would be wasting quality tea and time.

The principle behind the art of brewing tea is to master the basic technique and to understand the characteristics of the three intrinsic components of brewing tea: tea leaves, water and the tea set. Through this, one would learn the best possible method of brewing to maximize the fragrance of the tea. Brewing tea is an art. Each minute detail unfolds the brewer's personality. Every step should be gracious and polished. For example, use the tea cloth only to dry the tea set, never to wipe the table. While serving tea, never hold the teacup at the rim. This reflects friendliness and respect. A guest would feel slighted if the offered teacup is held in a place where his lips are meant to touch. Therefore, while learning the art of brewing tea, it is important to learn etiquette too. It is only thus that both you and your guest will fully enjoy the pleasure of drinking tea.

In conclusion, learning the art of brewing tea is to learn to brew tea with sophistication, ease and panache.

The glowing sunset warms the grasslands
A freshly brewed cup of scented Pu-erh warms the hands
Life is of such simple pleasures

Fun with Tea Amid Nature

In the lap of lush greens fields
The summer blooms carpet the ground in riotous glory
A wild chrysanthemum
The perfect adornment for the rustic tea table

Brewing tea out in the country is no trouble
In fact, the fresh water and air is perfect for its aroma
Result… a memorable rustic experience

Tea in the Countryside

Part 1

The Art Is in the Details

To brew a good pot of tea and enjoy a cup of fragrant tea is a process consisting of numerous minor details. Mastering these details ensures the superior quality of the brewed tea. Fine appreciation of this process reflects character and personality of the person brewing the tea.

A Master Tea Brewer Focuses on the Details

According to tea culture expert Mr. Kou Dan, “The fine art of brewing tea lies in the technique of brewing a good pot of tea and the appreciation of a cup of tea.” Tea is an integral part of everyone’s life. If the tea is only to quench thirst, one only needs to boil a handful of tea leaves. However, if you are looking for spiritual satisfaction, brewing tea becomes a form of art that requires skill, time and mood. The entire process of brewing tea—choosing the tea leaves, selecting the type of water, choosing the tea set—should be an enjoyable one, leading to the true appreciation of the tea. To become a connoisseur of tea, one must first master the technique of brewing a quality pot of tea.

Regardless of whether you are brewing a pot of tea for yourself or for a social gathering pay particular attention to the details. This will ensure a final brew of exceptional fragrance and quality tea. Elegant execution reflects one’s taste and character. The attention to details reflects one’s breeding. The art of drinking and brewing tea is in fact a process of self-improvement and personal cultivation.

Preparation Details

Posture

We are usually seated during the process of brewing tea. Sit upright. Keep legs naturally aligned and straight, either forming a 90 degree right angle with the floor or slightly angled. If seated on a sofa, or a slightly lower chair, keep legs naturally aligned and angled either to the left or right. Keep shoulders back, appearing both tall and alert.

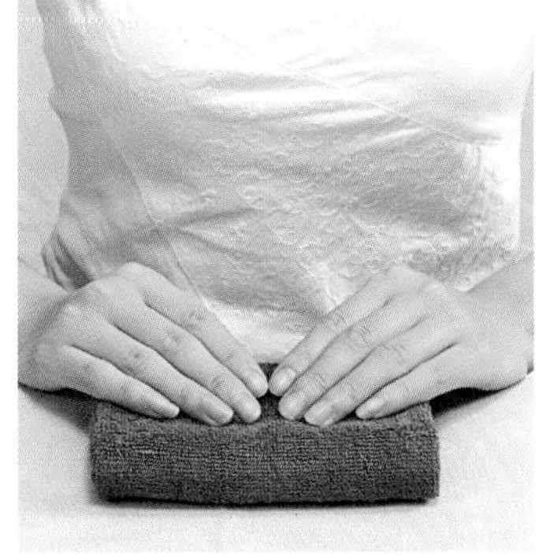

↑ Place hands lightly on the tea towel.

Hands

The process of brewing tea involves our hands. Therefore, eyes usually are focused on the hands of the person brewing the tea. The mood, confidence, breeding of the person brewing the tea is all reflected through the "expressions" of the hands. Professional tea servers usually have beautiful and well-cared for hands.

When the hands are at rest, either cross hands and place them on the lap or rest them lightly on the tea towel. Too-relaxed shoulders or fluttering hands appear coarse and inelegant.

↑ Place crossed hands on the lap.

Attire

Comfort is the first consideration when choosing the attire. It should not be too formal or too casual. If you choose to wear a long dress or jacket, be sure to tuck the skirt while sitting. Remember to pull the sleeves back as well in case it hampers you during the process of brewing the tea.

Reminders:

- Do not cross or stretch your legs when seated; you may accidentally kick someone.
- When sitting, take up only half or two-thirds of the seat. Do not take up the entire seat, or lean back on the chair.
- Do not wear too many accessories on your hands or wrists.
- Ensure that your nails are clean and well-shaped. Wash your hands before brewing tea. Avoid scented hand moisturizer and perfume.

Environment

People who enjoy drinking tea prefer a clean and comfortable environment. Whether the background is Oriental or Western is inconsequential. The ambience is the most important factor for a tea connoisseur.

Music

Some people like to listen to music while brewing tea. Light and soothing music such as zither, guqin, flute, violin or piano pieces are all suitable accompaniments. Light music relaxes the mind and creates a soothing atmosphere. However, music is not mandatory. The choice of music depends on personal preferences and habits.

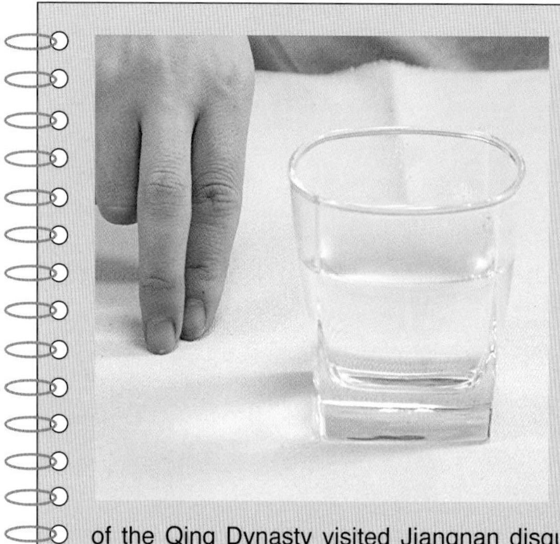

★ Tea Tips ★

Bend knuckles in respect

When someone offers tea or pours tea for you, join the second and third fingers of the right hand together, bend them slightly and lightly knock the table twice in thanks. This etiquette, unique to the art of tea, has several stories associated with its origin. A popular version says that once Emperor Qianlong of the Qing Dynasty visited Jiangnan disguised as a servant. When he entered a roadside teahouse, the owner, handed him the teapot to serve tea to the eunuch disguised as his master. Unable to betray his emperor, the nervous eunuch joined the second and third fingers of his right hand, bent them slightly and lightly knocked the table twice, as a sign of kneeling down to show respect. This particular etiquette slowly spread among the people. Today, irrespective of age or station in life, lightly knocking the table twice in thanks is a custom. Bending the fingers is not essential; simply knocking the table lightly is enough to convey friendliness and respect.

Key Points for Brewing Tea

Selection and Setting of the Tea Set

Choosing the right tea set and its arrangement is very important. Use both hands in coordination when handling the tea set, and place each item back to its original setting after use. The setting can be in the order of the brewer's preference and convenience. For example, the teapot can be placed on either side. However, if the item is placed on the right side, reach for it with the right hand, if it is on the left hand, use the left hand. Transfer if necessary. Avoid reaching across items.

↑ Use a covered tea bowl for brewing Tieguanyin tea.

↑ Use a Zisha tea set for brewing Dahongpao tea.

↑ Use a porcelain cup for brewing White Peony Tea.

↑ Use a covered tea bowl for brewing Long Jing tea.

Dos and Don'ts:

× Avoid reaching across the table; don't use your right hand to reach for items on the left.

× Avoid reaching across other items. For example, don't reach across the teacups for the tea jar.

√ If something is on the left side, use your left hand and than transfer. After use, place it back.

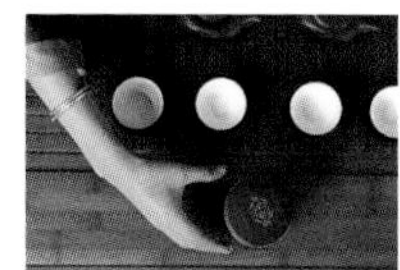

√ If the item is in a corner, reach around the other items to get it.

Taking Out Tea Leaves

The amount of tea leaves used depends on need. After use, seal the tea jar properly before replacing it. (In case of green tea leaves, refrigerate the jar.) If there are unused tea leaves on the tea plate, do not put it back in the tea jar. Tea leaves absorb moisture from the air causing oxidization. Putting it back into the tea jar will affect the quality of the tea leaves.

Taking out dry tea

↑ Use a teaspoon to gently sweep loose tea leaves onto the tea place.

↑ Use a tea scoop to scoop tea leaves that are not too brittle.

Tea Towel

The tea towel is essential to the process of tea brewing. It is used in wiping both the exterior of the tea set and the water or tea stains at the base. Choose towels that are highly absorbent when buying tea towels.

Folding the tea towel

Method 1:

↑ Demarcate the towel into three equal parts, and fold from both ends.

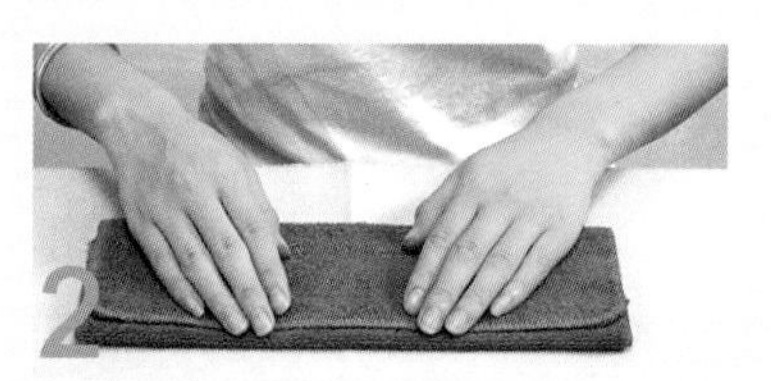

↑ Demarcate the folded towel into three equal parts.

↑ Fold again inward twice and smoothen it.

↑ Place the towel seam side facing the tea brewer.

Method 2:

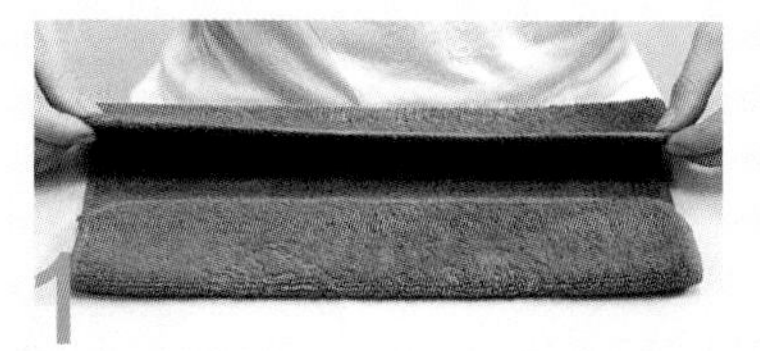

↑ Demarcate the tea towel into four equal parts and fold the two ends inward, aligned with the middle line.

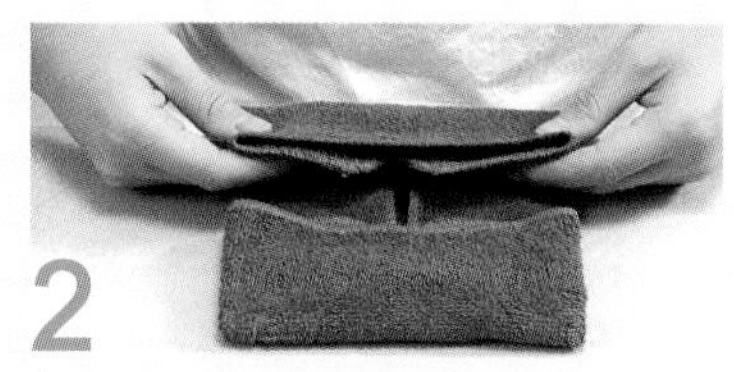

↑ Demarcate the folded towel in four equal parts again and repeat.

↑ Fold the folded towel into two and smoothen it.

↑ Place the towel seam side facing the tea brewer.

Using the tea towel

Lift the towel with both hands, thumbs on top and the remaining four fingers below. Free the right hand to hold the item to be cleaned.

↑ Lift the towel with both hands, thumbs on top and the remaining four fingers below.

↑ Release the towel end in the right hand and pick the item to be cleaned.

↑ Wipe the bottom of the Gongdao cup.

↑ Use the tea towel to wipe the bottom of the teacups.

↑ Use the tea towel to wipe the bottom of the teapot.

Dos and Don'ts:

- Avoid using the tea towel as a dishcloth. The tea towel's purpose is to dry the exterior of the tea set or mop the water or tea stains at the base of the tea set. However, water or tea stains on the tray or table should be cleaned with other towels. Using the tea towel to clear discarded fruit peels off the table is a sign of disrespect to the guests.
- Avoid using wet tea towels. Ensure that the tea towel is dry before using.
- Avoid using tea towels that are frayed, scruffy or dyed towels.

Warming the Tea Glass

Plain and transparent glass is widely used to brew tea in order to allow the tea drinker to admire the "dance of the tea leaves." Its thick base can withstand high temperatures. The volume of the glass cup should be approximately between 150–200ml. Whether you are warming the cup or offering the tea, hold the cup with both hands.

↑ Support the base of the cup with one hand and wrap the other hand around the mid section.

Holding the teacup

The three methods of warming the cup:

Method 1:

↑ Hold the cup as level as possible, ensuring that the water in the cup doesn't spill out. Turn the cup anticlockwise—to the front, to the left, to the back and to the right in one full circle.

↑ Pour the water from the cup into the basin.

★ Tea Tips ★

The warming procedure and way of holding the teacup for handleless, tube-shaped small porcelain teacups is similar to that of the glass teacup.

Method 2:

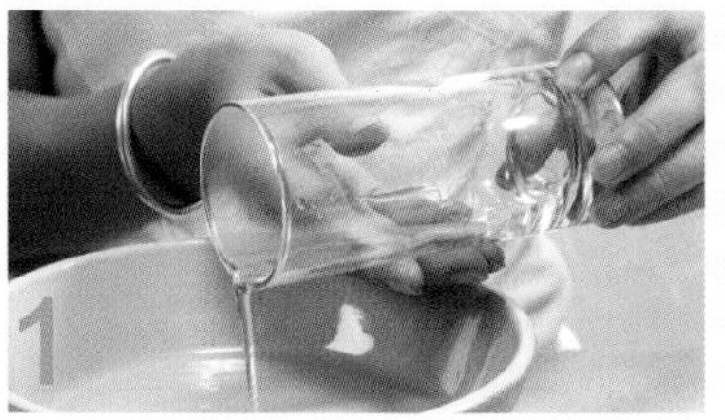

↑ Hold the body of the cup with the right hand and support its base with the left, positioning it levelly.

↑ Turn the cup inward with the left hand, and tilt it slowly. Pour the water into the basin.

Method 3:

↑ Place the cup level on the palm of the right hand and roll it inward with the left hand.

↑ At the same time, tilt the cup and pour the water inside into the basin.

Reminders:

Avoid touching the rim of the cup when warming the cup.

↑ The fresh aroma of tea is even detectable from the lid of the tea bowl.

Heating the Tea Bowl

The tea bowl is also known as "the bowl of three elements." The lid represents the sky; the saucer represents the earth while the tea bowl itself represents man. Therefore, brewing tea in a tea bowl represents the merging of the sky, earth and human beings amid the sweet fragrance of the tea. We cannot use the lid, bowl and saucer separately. Putting aside the saucer and lid to use only the tea bowl for brewing tea, is not only inappropriate and inelegant, but also very impolite.

When brewing tea in a covered tea bowl, you can inhale the fragrance from both the lid and the tea liquid. There is more information on using the tea bowl for aroma and tea appreciation in the chapter Jasmine Tea.

Warming the tea bowl

↑ Hold the base of the bowl with the left hand and the lid with the right hand. Turn the bowl anticlockwise for one full circle (similar to the glass cup).

→ Take off the lid of the bowl and hold it at an angle to the bowl. Drain the water in the bowl into the basin against the lid, slowly turning the lid with the right hand.

Handling the Teapot

Handling the teapot is not an easy task. It requires technique to hold the teapot comfortably without getting scalded. Handle the teapot with such ease that even others feel comfortable.

The correct way to handle the teapot

Hold the handle with the thumb and third finger and lift the teapot, lightly pressing the lid of the teapot with the second finger. Make sure not to block the air hole. Press the fourth finger against the handle and tuck in the little finger.

Holding the teapot with both hands

A beginner can choose to hold the teapot with both hands. Press the top of the lid with the third finger of one hand, and hold the handle of the teapot with the thumb, second finger and third finger of the other hand.

Other ways of handling the teapot

↑ Hook the handle of the teapot with the third finger and hold it tightly using the thumb. Tuck in the fourth and last finger and lightly press the second finger on the top of the teapot.

↑ Hook the handle with the second and third finger. Lightly press the thumb on the top of the teapot.

Dos and Don'ts:

- While brewing tea, avoid placing the teapot such that the spout faces the guest.
- Never block the air hole on the lid.

Placing the teapot lid

↑ Lift the lid and place it on the tea tray.

↑ Lean it against the side rim of the tea tray.

↑ Keep it in a designated place.

★ Tea Tips ★

Use porcelain, clay or glass teapots in the same way as Zisha teapots. Choose a tea set with care; always choose a size and weight that is easy to handle.

Fairness Cup and Strainer

↑ The fairness cup holds the tea before it is poured into individual teacups. This lends a uniform flavor to the tea.

↑ The strainer, placed on top, prevents the tea leaves from falling into the cup. When not in use, place on its stand or against the tea tray.

↑ If the fairness cup has a straining device then the strainer is unnecessary.

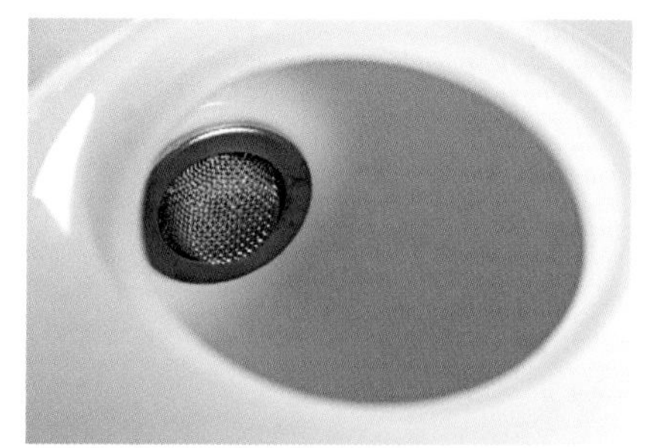

↑ If the teapot has a straining device then the strainer is unnecessary.

★ Tea Tips ★

The strainer is frequently blocked by tea dust and tea dregs. Therefore, clean and rinse carefully after use.

Aroma Cup and Tea Appreciation Cup

The aroma cup and tea appreciation cup are sometimes used to brew Oolong tea.

Warming the cup

↑ Hold the tea appreciation cup in one hand and turn it anticlockwise. →

↑ Pour the water in the cup onto the tea tray.

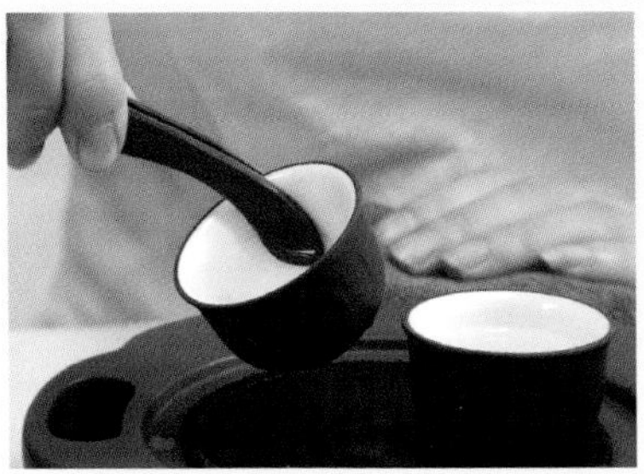

↑ Use tea tongs to hold the tea appreciation cup and turn it anticlockwise for a full circle before draining the water.

↑ Use tea tongs to pick up the aroma cup and warm it the same way as the tea appreciation cup.

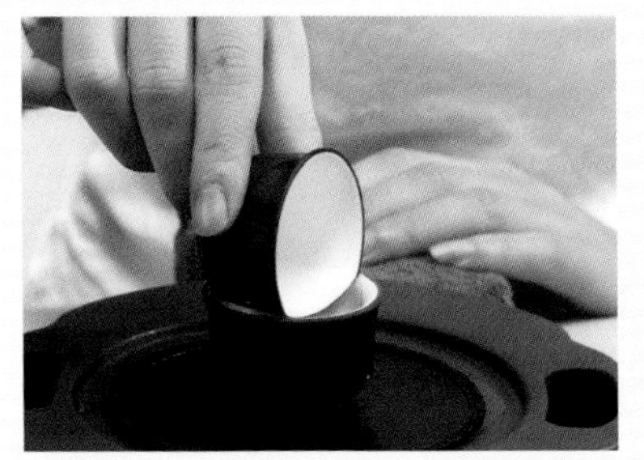

↑ Warm the cup by stacking them one on top of the other. Roll the cups between the fingers to warm them.

↑ Use tea tongs to pick up the tea appreciation cup to warm another cup.

Aroma appreciation

↑ Pour the tea in the tea appreciation cup, hold the empty aroma cup to breathe in the fragrance.

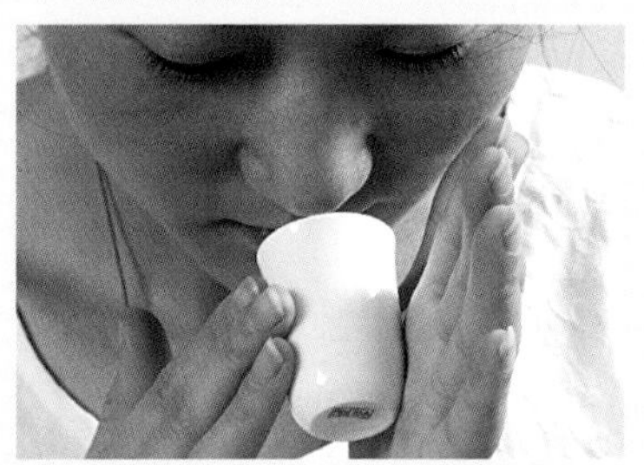

↑ Rub the aroma cup between your hands and bring it toward your nose to breathe in the fragrance.

Tea appreciation

↑ Hold the cup between the thumb and second finger, support the base with the third finger, tuck in the fourth and last finger and hold the tea appreciation cup steady.

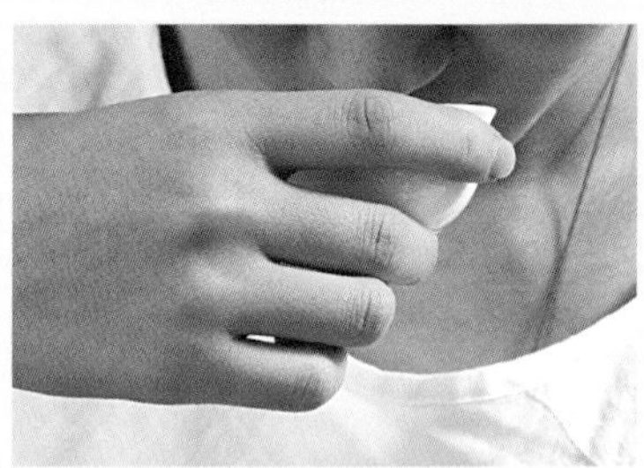

↑ Slowly bring the cup to your lips and gently sip the tea, inhale the fragrance.

Six Helpers in the Art of Tea (also known as the extended tea set or tea props)

These items of an extended tea set aid in brewing tea. They make the entire tea brewing process cleaner and more elegant. When picking up these items, avoid touching the areas that come in contact with the tea.

Tea funnel

↑ Place on the teapot to expand the opening. This will avoid spilling tea or water.

Teaspoon

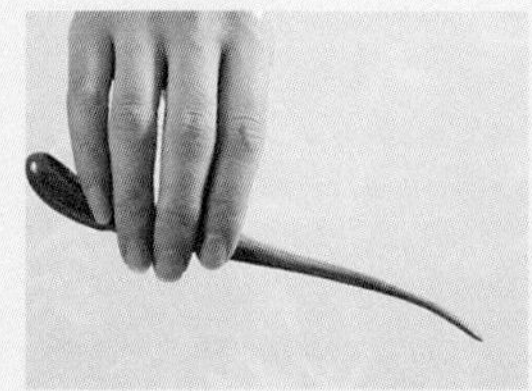

↑ Use to spoon tea leaves from the tea jar. Be gentle and slow.

Tea tongs

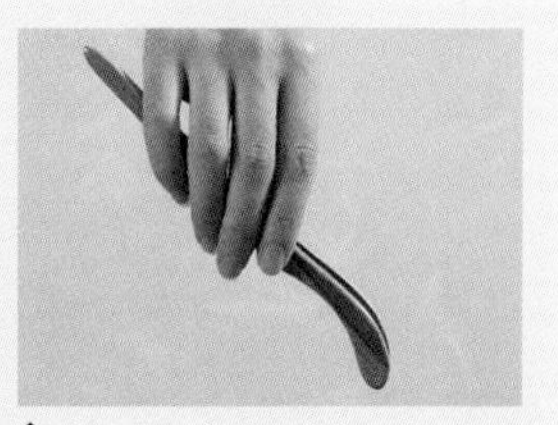

↑ Use to warm teacups and when picking up tea appreciation cups and aroma cups for guests.

Tea scoop	Tea pick	Yanghu Brush

↑ To pick up large amount of non-brittle tea leaves.	↑ Use to unblock the spout of the teapot.	↑ Use to clean the exterior of the teapot. This helps maintain and preserve the color and texture of the teapot which comes with age.

Dos and Don'ts:

Don't touch the six helpers in the art of tea where they come in contact with the tea.

Tea plate

The tea plate is used to keep the dry tea leaves. It is used to display the tea leaves during tea art performances. Avoid touching the edge of the plate with your hands when picking up the tea leaves.

↑ Hold the tea plate firmly with fingers of one hand, support its base with the other hand.

↓ Tilt the tea plate and gently sweep the tea leaves into the teapot.

★ Tea Tips ★

Use small unscented porcelain, wooden or bamboo containers or saucers as tea plates.

Tea knife

When brewing compressed tea leaves, such as tea bricks or tea discs, it is necessary to use the tea knife.

↑ Slide the tea knife into the tea discs at an angle.

↑ Press the handle of the tea knife down to dislodge the tea leaves.

↑ Press the thumb on the tea leaves to pick up the dislodged tea leaves.

"Brewing from High" and "Serving from Low"

"Brewing from High"

"Brewing from high" is a distinctive method of pouring water during the process of brewing tea. There are three ways of pouring water. In the first, boiling water is directly poured into the teacup until it is seven-tenth full or the teapot is full. In the second method, one pours the water either anticlockwise or clockwise. In the third method, "the phoenix dips its head thrice," circle up and down three times in rhythm. Ensure that the amount of water poured is just right and not a drop is wasted. This movement is a show of respect to the guest. Usually the water is poured from a height. The force of the water scatters the tea leaves, causing the flavor of the tea to be distributed more evenly.

↑ Brew from high.

↑ Serve from low.

"Serving from Low"

When serving the tea, it is best to pour from a low height. The fairness cup or the teapot should be held slightly higher than the rim of the teacup, but it should not touch the rim. The purpose is to avoid losing the fragrance of the tea or spilling the tea. Hold the tea towel with one hand, and pick up the fairness cup or the teapot with the other. If the spout of the fairness cup or the teapot is wet, wipe it immediately. It is impolite to let tea drip into a cup. Wipe the spout after serving each cup.

↑ Wipe the spout of the fairness cup or the teapot after serving every cup.

A Half-cup of Tea; A Full Cup of Wine

When serving tea, the appropriate amount is to fill only seven-tenth of the cup. Filling the cup to the brim is considered impolite. Even the second cup of tea should be seven-tenth full. When using aroma cups and the tea appreciation cups, first distribute the tea into each aroma cup before swirling it around and pouring it into the tea appreciation cup. Avoid overflowing.

Tea Distribution

In other to ensure that the flavor of the tea is distributed evenly, first pour the tea into the fairness cup before distributing it in each tea appreciation cup. Pour the tea directly from the teapot in a sweeping arc motion to ensure the even distribution of the flavor—this is known as "General Guan touring the city walls." The residual essence of tea in the teapot should also be evenly distributed into each individual cup a drop at a time—this is known as "Han Xin inspecting the troops."

★ Tea Tips ★

General Guan touring the city walls, Han Xin inspecting the troops

General Guan and Han Xin are historical figures of different dynasties. One often hears the phrases "General Guan touring the city walls" and "Han Xin inspecting the troops" following consecutively. In the early days, people used the so-called "Chaoshan four treasures," namely, the Chaoshan stove (to light a fire in the mud stove), the jade book (to boil water in a clay pot), the Mengchen teapot (to brew the tea) and the Ruochen cup(to drink the tea). The amount of tea leaves added was usually very large. The pot would usually be 70–80% full. Therefore, the tea brewed was very strong. To distribute the flavor evenly, the teacups were arranged either in a straight line or in the form of a pyramid and swept across the cups in a smooth motion while pouring the tea. This move was known as "General Guan touring the city walls." The last drops of tea have the strongest flavor. It is known as the essence of the tea and must be evenly distributed—one drop per cup. This was known as "Han Xin inspecting the troops."

A Master Tea Brewer's Three-step Formula

step 1: Pre-brewing Preparation

There are three things that we should take note of before beginning the brewing process.

First, prepare the tea leaves. Take out an appropriate amount of tea leaves as per the number of guests. Next boil water—different tea requires water of different temperature. Avoid re-boiling water. Also, one must make sure that the amount of water poured into the kettle is enough. Lastly, prepare the needed tools or condiments in accordance to the type of tea brewed. For example, when brewing black tea, one should keep sugar cubes and cream.

step 2: Brewing

A tea-brewing expert pays close attention to three aspects: water temperature, quantity of tea leaves and brewing time. The water temperature for different tea types vary. For example, Oolong tea should be brewed in boiling water. Green tea requires about 80°C. The amount of tea leaves varies in accordance to the taste of the guests. When brewing tea in a cup, the ratio of tea to water is usually 1:50; in a pot, the ratio changes depending on the type of tea leaves and the preferences of the tea drinker. Finally, as tea leaves are produced in different places and harvested at different times, the time for brewing varies. Usually, tea brewed in a cup is ready after steeping for 2 to 3 minutes. However, some teas may take longer. For example, White Peony Tea requires steeping for 5 minutes. Also, tea brewed in a pot is steeped for different time lengths. For example, the first infusion of Oolong tea is very short, needing only approximately 40 seconds. Subsequent infusions take a little longer.

step 3: Cleaning and storing the tea set after use

Clean and store the tea set immediately after use. Tea dregs left in the teapot over an extended period of time begin to rot. This will cause the flavor of the tea being lost in subsequent brewing. Also, tea dust accumulates easily on the tea set. Do not use dishwashing detergents to clean Zisha teapots because the teapot will absorb the chemicals present, thus affecting the quality of the tea. Drain the tea dregs and wash the Zisha teapot with plain water. Porcelain or glass items can be cleaned with dishwashing detergents. Ensure that the handles, base and inner walls are cleaned. Use soft materials such as cotton cloths in cleaning. Metal mesh or other hard materials will scratch the glazed surface of these items. Dry with the tea towel. The tea towel should also be washed and dried. Lastly, ensure safety by turning off all electrical appliances. Take extra care in caring for the tea set. For example, bamboo or wooden tea trays tend to crack and leak if it is not used frequently during dry seasons. Cover it with a moist towel.

★ Tea Tips ★

The selection of the tea set is very important. The taste and fragrance of different tea leaves vary when brewed in different tea sets.

Column 1

The Tea Family

From a Bitter Plant "Tu" to "Cha" (Tea)

The custom of drinking tea originated from the time of Prince Zhou of the state of Lu. Commonly believed to have been first used as a medicine, it later evolved into a drink. Originally known as "tu," after the bitter edible plant, it was also called "ming." The name "cha" first replaced "tu" during the mid-Tang Dynasty and is commonly used today.

Teas are usually named after their place of origin. Examples include Qimen Black Tea, West Lake Long Jing, Huangshan Maofeng, etc. They are also named after their shapes, such as Queshe (sparrow tongue). The ones named after the tea trees they are harvested from are Dahongpao, Tieguanyin, etc. The ones named after the season they are harvested in are Yuqian Cha (harvested before rain), Mingqian Cha (harvested before the Qingming festival), Qiu Cha (Autumn Tea) or Dongpian (Winter Tea). Named after fermentation, there is the "fully fermented tea," the "half-fermented tea" and the "non-fermented tea." "Border sales tea," "exported tea," "domestic sales tea," "foreign sales tea," etc., derive their names from their area of sale.

Tea Leaves Classifications

Chinese tea leaves can be classified into two major types. (1) Basic tea leaves are freshly picked and processed before being made into green tea, black tea, Oolong tea, yellow tea, white tea and dark tea. (2) Reprocessed tea leaves are treated and reprocessed basic tea leaves made into flower tea, compressed tea, tea extracts, fruit tea, herbal tea, tea bags or tea flavored drinks, etc.

Basic Tea Varieties

Variety	Species
Green Tea	West Lake Long Jing, Dongting Bi Luo Chun, Huangshan Maofeng, Liu'an Guapian, etc.
Black Tea	Dianhong, Qihong, Ninghong, Yihong, Minhong, etc.
Oolong Tea	Dahongpao, Tieguanyin, Fenghuang Dancong, Dongding Oolong, etc.
Yellow Tea	Junshan Silver Needles, Mengting Huangya, Guishan Maojian, Huoshan Huang Dacha, etc.
White Tea	Baihao Silver Needles, White Peony, Gongmei, Shoumei, etc.
Dark Tea	Biancha, Pu-erh, Liubao, etc.

Green tea

Green tea is a type of unfermented tea, easily recognized by its green leaves and tea liquid. There are two types of green tea— quality green tea and mainstream green tea . Quality green tea is usually hand produced in limited quantity. Examples include West Lake Long Jing, Dongting Bi Luo Chun, etc. When brewed in a glass teacup, one can admire the leaves unfurl in a "dance of tea leaves." The shape of the tea leaves can be differentiated into twisted, flat-shaped, spiral-shaped and various other shapes. Mainstream green tea is usually mass-produced by machines. The quality is of mid to low standard, usually made for export. A certain amount is used to fumigate flower teas. Sun-dried green tea is mostly used to produce compressed tea.

Black tea

Black tea is a type of fully fermented tea. Its black tea leaves and liquid is easily recognizable. It can be further classified as Gongfu Black Tea, Broken Black Tea and Small Species Black Tea. Gongfu Black Tea is the traditional Chinese black tea. Known varieties include Yunnan's Dianhong Gongfu, Anhui's Keemun Gongfu, etc. Broken Black Tea requires simultaneous kneading and cutting, thus the final product are grainlike tea leaves, usually sold internationally. Small Species Black Tea is the earliest form of black tea. The Zhengshan Small Species Black Tea is of the best quality.

Oolong tea

Oolong tea can be classified according to its place of production—Southern Min Oolong, Northern Min Oolong, Guangdong Oolong and Taiwan Oolong. Northern Min Oolong's degree of fermentation is stronger; it is straight and coarse. Sometimes, the end is twisted. The leaves are edged black. Thirty percent of the leaf is black and seventy percent is green. Examples include Wuyi Narcissus, Wuyi Cassia, etc.

Column 1 

Southern Min Oolong's fermentation is lighter. It is circular and twisted; each leaf is edged black. Examples include Tieguanyin, Yellow Osmanthus, etc. Guangdong Oolong's degree of fermentation is heavier than Southern Min Oolong. Its shape is tight and firm. The leaves are bigger and coarser. The bottom of the leaves is yellowish-green with a defined black edge. Examples include Fenghuang Dancong, Lingtou Dancong, etc. The fragrance is unique and varies according to the plant. Taiwan Oolong is the type of Oolong tea that is least fermented. Those that are more heavily fermented include Dongding Oolong, Jinxuan Oolong, etc. They are shaped like a half ball and the leaves are green on the underside. The most heavily fermented tea is the Baihao Oolong, also known as Champagne Oolong or Eastern Beauty.

Yellow tea

Yellow tea is lightly fermented tea. Yellow tea is differentiated by the tenderness of their tea leaves when they are picked and can be classified by their yellow tea bud, such as Junshan Silver Needles, or Yellow Xiaocha, such as Guishan Maojian, or Yellow Dacha, such as Huoshan Huang Dacha.

White tea

White tea is lightly fermented tea. Its tea liquid is pale and the flavor mellow and sweet. The well-known varieties include Baohao Silver Needles, White Peony, etc.

Dark tea

Dark tea is a post-fermented tea. Varieties include Hu'nan dark tea, Sichuan Biancha, Yunnan Pu-erh, Guangxi Liubao Cha, etc. It is usually compressed tea, such as tea discs, tea bricks, Tuo-cha, etc. There are also bar-shaped teas. In the past, dark tea was mainly sold in areas such as Tibei, Xinjiang and Inner Mongolia which are mainly occupied by the minorities. A small percentage is exported overseas. Therefore, dark tea is also known as border sales tea. Dark tea is mostly of lower quality, but it does not spoil easily and has a unique flavor. Of the varieties of dark tea, Pu-erh tea is especially renowned internationally and is growing in popularity.

Re-processed Tea Varieties

Variety	Species
Flower Tea	Jasmine Tea, Zhulan Tea, Rose Tea, etc.
Compressed Tea	Black Brick, Rice Brick, Tuo-cha, etc.
Extracted Tea	Instant Tea, Tea Polyphenol
Fruit Tea	Lychee Tea, Lemon Tea, etc.
Herbal tea	Diet Tea, Relaxant Tea
Teabags	Black Teabags, Green Teabags, Oolong Teabags, etc.
Tea-flavored drinks	Tea-flavored Coca-Cola, Tea-flavored Sodas, etc.

In addition, tea is widely used in the processed food industry. It is made into many tea-flavored foods, such as tea-flavored melon seeds, tea-flavored jelly, tea-flavored moon cakes, tea-flavored ice pops, etc. Everyday chemical industry products such as toothpaste, make-up, facial cleansers, facial masks, shower gels and shampoos, etc. also contain tea extracts.

Tea That Isn't Tea

When parts of a plant, such as the root, stem, leaf, flower or fruit is used in brewing or made into a drink, people commonly call that drink a form of tea. For example, Chinese dates, lemon or haws are known as fruit teas. Buckwheat and barley are known as grain tea. Flowers such as chrysanthemum, rose and golden lotus are known as flower teas. Herbs such as broadleaf holly, eucommia bark or wolfberry are also made into tea. These varying forms of tea can be brewed together with tea leaves or can be brewed on their own. Two or more varieties can be brewed together too, such as Chrysanthemum Pu-erh tea and Chrysanthemum Haw Green Tea, etc.

Part 2

Brewing Tea with Ease

Drinking tea is a time of relaxation. Once familiar with the details and process of brewing tea, with the added knowledge of tea characteristics and the features of the tea set, brewing tea becomes easy and fun.

Crystal Clear Green Tea

Green Tea Production

Picking fresh leaves

↓

Pan-drying

↓

Rolling and shaping the leaves

↓

Drying the leaves

Basic Green Tea Knowledge

Methods of brewing	The three different methods of brewing
Water temperature	Should be around 80°
The ratio of leaves to water	1:50
Appropriate tea sets	Includes glass or porcelain teacup (teapot)

Green Tea Facts

- Usually, when brewing tea, water is added to the tea leaves. However, when brewing green tea, there are three methods of brewing:
- High-quality green tea is made from tender and fine tea leaves. It is brewed in water temperature of 80°. Medium-quality tea leaves are made from a mixture of coarse and tender tea leaves; the temperature can be slightly higher, and it is usually brewed in 90°.
- The amount of the tea used depends on the grade of the tea leaves, the strength of the flavor and the preference of the tea drinker.
- Glass teacups are used for admiring the "dance of the tea leaves." They are usually small (volume of approximately 200 ml) with a heavy base.

Brewing Tips

- Convenience and courtesy are the most important factors when brewing green tea. Therefore, green tea is usually brewed in teacups.
- Because the water temperature requirement for green tea is between 80° and 90°, the water dispenser can be used.
- Different types of tea sets and different methods of brewing can be used for the same type of tea.

The Top Brewing Method: Bi Luo Chun

Pre-brewing Preparations

- Prepare the tea set: Kettle (the hot plate used for boiling water is a necessity and is not shown in the picture), glass teacup, tea towel, tea plate, teaspoon and basin.
- Pour the appropriate amount of water into the kettle and bring to boil. Let the temperature drop to 80° before use.
- Gently scoop the necessary amount of Bi Luo Chun tea leaves onto the tea plate with the teaspoon.

Brewing

1 Tea set

← Arrange the tea set to begin brewing.

★ Tea Tips ★

When warming the glass teacup, first rotate vertically before rotating it levelly. Finally, drain the water into the basin.

2 Warming the cup

↑ Pour a small amount of heated water into the cup.

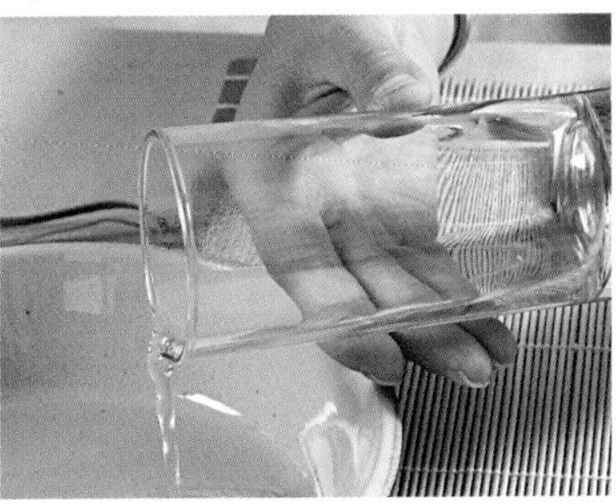

↑ Warm the teacup.

3 Pouring water

↑ Directly pour the water into the cup until it is 7/10 full.

4 Adding tea leaves

↑ Gently sweep the dry Bi Luo Chun tea leaves into the glass teacup.

5 Admiring the "dance of the tea leaves"

↑ The tea buds slowly sink to the bottom of the cup upon absorbing the water.

↑ As the tea buds sink to the bottom, the liquid turns green. The effect, seen through the glass cup, is called "dance of the tea leaves."

Offering tea

→ Offer the freshly brewed Bi Luo Chun to the guests.

More Green Tea Information

- Top-grade green teas such as Bi Luo Chun, Jingshan Tea, Mengting Ganlu, etc. are usually more compact with fine and tender buds. To brew this tea, pour heated water into the cup until it is seven-tenth full. Add tea leaves.
- When entertaining guests at home, invite the guests to look at the dry tea leaves before brewing and again look at the wet tea leaves after brewing.

The Middle Brewing Method: West Lake Long Jing

Pre-brewing Preparation

- Prepare the tea set: Kettle, tea bowl, tea towel, tea scoop, basin and tea tray.
- Pour the appropriate amount of water into the kettle and bring to boil. Let the temperature cool to 80° before use.
- Gently scoop the necessary amount of West Lake Long Jing tea leaves onto the tea scoop with the teaspoon.

Brewing

1 Tea set

← Arrange the tea set to begin brewing.

2 Warming the cup

↑ Pour a small amount of heated water into the tea bowl.

↑ Warm the tea bowl.

↑ Warm the lid of the tea bowl.

3 Adding tea leaves

← Gently add the West Lake Long Jing tea leaves into the tea bowl.

4 Moisturizing tea leaves

↑ Pour a small amount of the water into the cup, just enough to soak the tea leaves.

↑ Watch the tea leaves slowly unfurl; it should take about 10 seconds.

5 Brewing

↑ Pour the water from a height until the cup is about 7/10 full and replace the lid.

↑ Place the lid at an angle to prevent stifling the yellow tea leaves.

Offering tea

→ Offer the freshly brewed cup of West Lake Long Jing to the guest on a saucer using both hands.

More Green Tea Information

- "Long Jing tea has a mellow flavor. Sweet but not saccharine, it leaves a fragrant aftertaste. Bland at first, it leaves a lingering ethereal taste," describes Lu Chiyun of the Qing Dynasty aptly. This describes not only Long Jing tea, but also all types of green tea.
- While brewing top-grade green tea, avoid covering the tea bowl immediately after adding water. Place lid at an angle to avoid stifling the yellow tea bud leaves.
- Fine and tender top-grade green teas such as flat-shaped, single bud-shaped, straight strips, curly strips, orchid-shaped or pearl-shaped are all suitable for the middle brewing method. First soak the tea leaves. While soaking, gently shake the cup. When the tea leaves have fully unfurled, add water until the cup is seven-tenth full. Alternatively, pour a small amount of water into the cup before adding the tea leaves. When the tea leaves have fully unfurled, add water until the cup is seven-tenth full.

The Bottom Brewing Method: Liu'an Guapian

Pre-brewing Preparation

- Prepare the tea set: Kettle, while porcelain teapot, tea towel, tea plate, coaster, tea appreciation cup, basin and teaspoon.
- Pour the appropriate amount of water into the kettle and bring to boil, let the temperature to drop to 85° before use.
- Gently scoop the necessary amount of Liu'an Guapian tea leaves onto the tea plate with the teaspoon.

Brewing

1 Tea set

↑ Arrange the tea set to begin brewing.

2 Warming the teapot

↑ Remove the teapot lid.

↑ Pour a small amount of heated water into the teapot.

↑ Pour the water from the teapot into the tea appreciation cup.

3 Adding tea leaves

↑ Gently add the Liu'an Guapian tea leaves into the teapot.

4 Pouring water

← Directly pour the heated water into the teapot until full, but avoid overflowing. Carefully replace the lid of the teapot and wait for 2 to 3 minutes.

5 Warming the cup

↑ Rotate the tea appreciation cup before draining the water into the basin.

6 Distributing tea

↑ Distribute the tea into each tea appreciation cup.

↑ Try to empty the teapot.

Offering tea

← Place the teacup on the saucer before offering the freshly brewed tea to the guests with both hands.

More Green Tea Information

- If using a teapot, select the right size. To brew two cups of tea, choose a smaller teapot having a volume of two cups. Or else, it would be necessary to use a fairness cup to ensure that the flavor of the tea is evenly distributed.
- Normal-grade green tea uses a mixture of rough and tender tea leaves that are more endurable. Despite their appearance, fragrance and taste, they are of a slightly lower quality than the top-grade green tea. When entertaining guests at home, use a small teapot to brew normal-grade tea leaves at approximately 90°. Be careful of the amount of tea leaves used and the tea brewed should be of an adequate flavor.
- The bottom brewing method of brewing tea requires adding the tea leaves before pouring the heated water.

Column 2

Water

Since the origin of tea, water and tea are two inseparable entities. Tea leaves need to be brewed in heated water. The quality of the water directly affects the quality of the tea. Therefore, identifying the quality of water is a necessary skill for any master tea brewer.

Historical Theories of Water

In his *Classic of Tea,* Lu Yu of the Tang Dynasty said, "Mountain water flowing over clear stones, or mineral springs are the best. Next is the remote river water. Well water, specially the ones used frequently, is of the lowest quality." People of the Song Dynasty emphasize five points when choosing the type of water for brewing tea—softness, clarity, sweetness, vitality (i.e., not stagnant) and low temperature. Ming Dynasty's Xu Cishu wrote in his tea manual, *Cha Shu,* "Water sets off the fragrance hidden in quality tea. Without water, there is no need to talk about tea." Ming Dynasty's Zhang Dafu further elaborates in his book *Meihua Caotang Bitan,* "The characteristics of tea will only be expressed with water. Even brewing substandard tea leaves with good quality water will give good quality tea. And, brewing good quality tea leaves in substandard water will give substandard tea." Without good quality water, no matter how good the tea leaves are, it will be impossible to brew sweet and fragrant tea.

Water Used in the Modern Day for Brewing Tea

Mineral water and purified water

It is naturally best to use spring water to brew tea. However, it is not easy to access spring water, especially in cities. Even if you live near a spring, it is likely to be polluted. Mineral water sold in supermarkets is a good substitute. Also, using a water purification system to remove the calcium and magnesium ions in mineral water will result in a better taste in brewing tea.

Purified water sold in the market is suitable. Tea brewed in this type of water is fragrant, fresh and pure.

Tap water

Tap water is the most commonly used water. Usually, the tap water provided by the city's water treatment plants meet the national chemical and hygiene drinking water requirements. However, chemicals such as chlorine that are frequently found in tap water will directly affect the taste and fragrance of the tea. The four easy steps listed below will reduce the effect of tap water on the taste of tea.

Water Purification System: Connect the tap water pipe to a purification system, or attach a water filter to the tap or the water dispenser.

Bamboo Charcoal: Add bamboo charcoal to the kettle when boiling water. (Bamboo Charcoal is sold at most tea shops.)

Extend the Boiling Time: Boil the water for an extended period to allow the chlorine to evaporate.

Tending the Water: Pour tap water into a clean container and leave it out in the open for 24 hours. After the chlorine has fully evaporated, boil it and use it to brew tea.

Boil Vital Water with Vital Fire

The heat used to boil water comes from many sources. Irrespective of the source, note the following: Firstly, boil on high temperature. Secondly, the source of fuel should be devoid of odors. Thirdly, do not re-boil, or it will affect the taste of the tea. When brewing tea at home, use electric fire or an alcoholic Bunsen burner if electric fire is not available.

Brewing different types of tea with the same type of water, or brewing the same type of tea with different types of water, or brewing different types of tea with different types of water will result in different tastes and aromas.

Column 2

More Information on Water

The best springs under the sky:

Beijing's Jade spring, Botu spring in Shandong's Ji'nan, Ningbiyu Spring in Yunn Anning, Yuye spring in Mt. Emei in Sichuan, the cold spring in Jiangsu's Zhengji and Gulian spring in the Kangwang Valley in Mt. Lu in Jiangxi are all renow springs. They are known as the best springs under the sky.

Second-best spring under the sky:

Huashan spring in Jiangsu's Wuxi falls under the second-best spring under the s

Water Anecdotes

Wang Anshi, the water connoisseur

Wang Anshi was not only an outstanding politician, but also a master in tea appreciation and a water connoisseur. He suffered from phlegm-heat retention in his old age. However, drinking Yangxian tea brewed in the water from Qutang Gorge, the second of the Three Gorges at Yangtze River, aided in relieving his illness. Once, Wang Anshi had requested Su Dongpo to bring him a jar of the water. Unfortunately, Su Dongpo only remembered this after his boat had passed the second gorge. So he scooped a jar of water from the third gorge. However, when Wang Anshi tasted the tea brewed in the water, he immediately knew that the water was not from Qutang Gorge. He explained that only the current in the second gorge was appropriate. The current in the first gorge was too strong, while the current in the third gorge was too slow. Therefore, when brewing Yangxian tea, the tea brewed in water from the first gorge is too strong, in water from the third gorge is too bland. Upon hearing this explanation, Su Dongpo was both impressed and remorseful.

Qianlong and Beijing's jade springs

Emperor Qianlong loved tea and was a water connoisseur. He believed that light-weight water was of the best quality. He used a custom-made silver chalice to measure the weight of the water of the same volume. Beijing's Jade Springs was conferred the title of "Best Spring under the Sky" after passing his silver chalice test. Qianlong was exceptionally partial to the waters of the Jade springs. However, the water loses its vitality after some time. Therefore, Qianlong came up with a method to revitalize the Jade Springs water. He poured the Jade springs water into a big and clean container, marking the water level. He then mixed an equal amount of water from other springs in the same container, leaving it to stand for some time. The unclean compounds sank to the bottom of the container. He separated the clear water on the top. The Jade Springs water being light, had risen to the top. It is believed that tea brewed by this water has a better taste.

Black Tea Production

Picking fresh leaves	Picking fresh leaves
↓	↓
Withering the leaves	Withering the leaves
↓	↓
Rolling and shaping the leaves	Rolling and shaping the leaves
↓	↓
Fermentation	Fermentation
↓	↓
Drying the leaves	Drying the leaves
↓	↓
Black tea	Broken black tea

Romantic Black Tea

Basic Black Tea Knowledge

Water temperature	Should be above 80°
Amount of tea leaves used	Brewing in a cup: the ratio of leaves to water should be 1:50
	2g/ per person
Brewing in a teapot	Appropriate tea sets include porcelain teapot (teacup), Zisha teapot (teacup)
Accompanying ingredients	Sugar, milk, honey, fruit juice, fruits such as lemons, coffee, brandy, etc.

Black Tea Facts

- When brewing black tea in a 200-ml teapot, use between 5g and 7g of tea leaves. When brewing broken black tea, increase to 6g to 8g. Black strip tea is suitable for drinking by itself. Broken black tea is suitable for flavored tea.
- Black strip tea can be brewed 3 to 5 times. Broken black tea can only be brewed 1 to 2 times, after which the tea leaves should be changed.
- Black tea has a rich and sharp flavor. Amateur drinkers may add a little sugar or honey.
- It is best to use white porcelain teapot or teacup to emphasize the vibrant color of the tea. Black tea sets can also double up as coffee sets.

Fresh tea leaves are green. Then how does tea turn black? Black tea is fully fermented tea leaves. Freshly picked tea leaves are put in withering troughs to allow them to wither, and thus lose their moisture. After this, the leaves are rolled and diced or shaped according to need. Next is the key process—fermentation. Finally, the leaves are dried to give black tea leaves. During the process, the chlorophyll in the fresh leaves oxidize and degrade, forming red polyphenols, such as theaflavins and thearubigins. Theaflavins are yellowish-orange in color whereas thearubigins are reddish. Both dissolve in the tea liquid. The other color compounds that do not dissolve in the tea liquid are brownish in color giving the characteristic black tea leaves and tea liquid.

Pure Black Tea: Keemun Gongfu Tea

Pre-brewing Preparation

- Prepare the tea set: Kettle, fairness cup, teapot, tea appreciation cup, basin, tea plate, teaspoon, tea towel and tea tongs.
- Pour suitable amount of water into the kettle and bring to boil.
- Scoop suitable amount of Keemun Gongfu Black Tea leaves onto the tea plate.

★ Tea Tips ★

If the tea set includes a teapot with a strainer, there is no need to use a strainer for the fairness cup.

Brewing

1 Tea set

← Arrange the tea set for brewing.

2 Warming the cup

↑ Pour the heated water into the teapot.

↑ Pour the water from the teapot into the fairness cup, and then into the tea appreciation cup.

3 Adding tea leaves

→ Gently scoop the Keemun Gongfu Black tea leaves into the teapot with the teaspoon.

4 Moisturizing tea leaves

↑ Pour a small amount of water into the teapot and quickly drain it in the basin.

↑ Quickly drain it in the basin.

5 Adding water

← Directly pour water into the teapot until full. Avoid overflowing. Steep for 2 to 3 minutes.

6 Warming the teacup

↑ Pick up the tea appreciation cup with the tea tongs.

↑ Drain the heated water in the teacup into the basin.

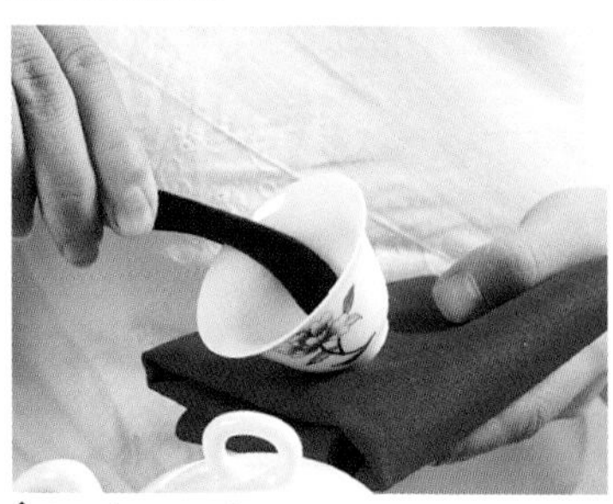

↑ Gently wipe the exterior and base of the teacup with the tea towel.

★ Tea Tips ★

If there is froth at the opening of the teapot, scrape it off with the teapot lid. The brewing method is similar to that of Oolong tea.

7 Readying the brew

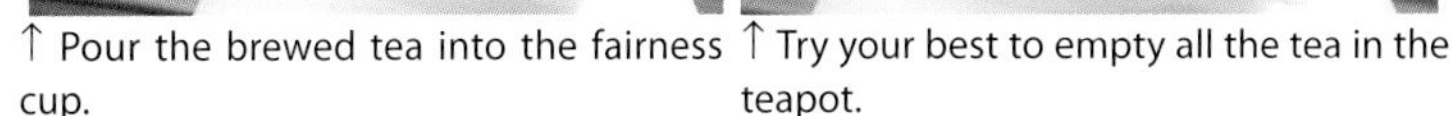

↑ Pour the brewed tea into the fairness cup.

↑ Try your best to empty all the tea in the teapot.

8 Distributing the tea

← Distribute the tea in the fairness cup into each individual tea appreciation cup.

Offering tea

→ Offer the tea to the guests with both hands.

More Black Tea Information

- The principle behind drinking pure black tea is to appreciate the fragrance and taste of black tea itself. It is only in drinking pure black tea that one can appreciate its unique flavor and charm of black tea.
- The tea leaves of Keemun Gongfu Black Tea are compact and thin with sharp ends. They are black and shiny, like a "jewel gleam." The flavor is rich and strong. The tea liquid is bright red with a honeyed fragrance. Aged Gongfu Black Tea has a good flavor if it is well preserved. Internationally, Keemun Gongfu Tea is ranked among the three top fragrant black teas together with India's Darjeeling Tea and Sri Lanka's Uva Black Tea.

Flavored Black Tea:
Milk Tea

Pre-brewing Preparation

- Prepare the tea set: Kettle, tea towel, tea plate, sugar bowl, milk cup and saucer, teacup and saucer and spoon. Warm both the milk cup and teacup.
- Pour suitable amount of water in the kettle and bring to boil. Heat fresh milk and pour it in the milk cup.
- Place two tea bags (one per cup) on the tea plate. Place sugar cubes on the sugar plate.

Brewing

1 Tea set

↑ Arrange the tea set for brewing.

2 Adding water

↑ Directly pour the water into the teacup.

3 Adding tea bags

↑ Put the tea bag in the teacup and steep for 1 to 2 minutes.

↑ Pick up the tea bag by the attached cotton string and swirl lightly to allow the liquid to fully soak up the flavor of the tea.

4 Adding milk

↑ Add heated milk into the cup.

5 Adding sugar

↑ Add a single cube of sugar into the cup.

Offering tea

← When offering tea to the guests, place the spoon as shown in the picture below. Never place the spoon inside the cup.

More Black Tea Information

- Use fresh milk for best fragrant taste. For best results, heat the milk before using. However, cold milk will also do.
- The ratio of milk to tea is usually 1:10. However, this can be adjusted according to preference. Sugar is also optional.
- When brewing flavored black tea, it is best to use broken black tea leaves for convenience and speed. The tea leaves in the tea bags are broken black tea leaves. These tea leaves were diced when processed, therefore, the soluble compounds in the tea leaves are released quickly when immersed, and the tea will be ready in a shorter period of time.
- The correct brewing method for tea bags is to add the tea bag to the water. Leave the attached cotton string out of the cup. If the tea bag is added first before pouring the water, the air in the teabag will cause the teabag to float up and this will affect the fragrance and taste of the tea. Also, the cotton string and label might fall into the cup when pouring the water.
- When milk is added to the broken black tea, the liquid turns dark red. This is a sign of good quality. If it turns ginger yellow, then the tea leaves are of substandard quality. If it turns grayish or a muddy cream color, then the tea leaves are of a more inferior quality.

Flavored Black Tea:
Lemon Tea

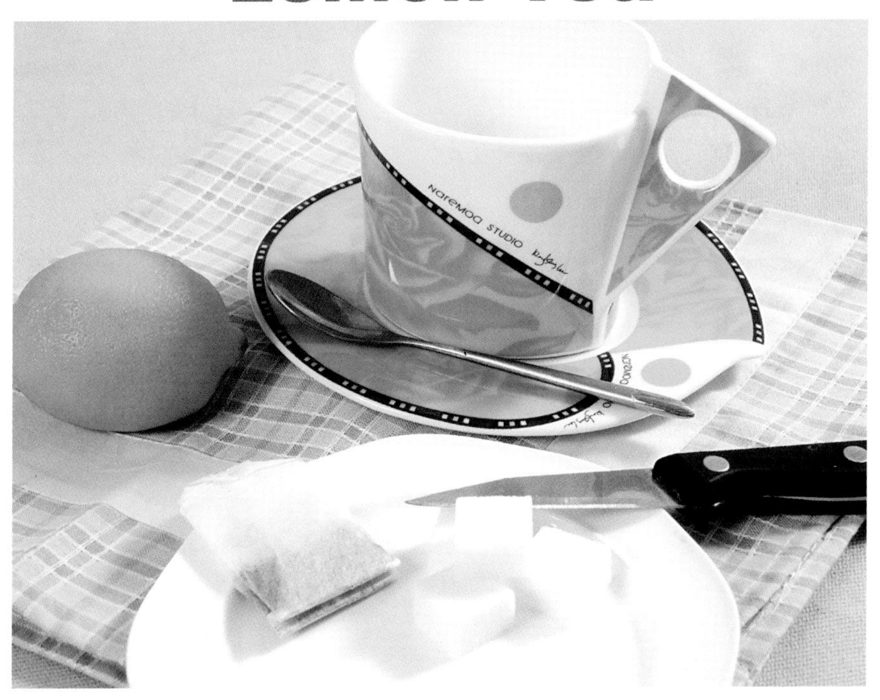

Pre-brewing Preparation

- Prepare the tea set: Kettle, teacup and saucer, spoon, fruit knife, lemon, sugar cubes and fruit plate. Warm the teacup.
- Pour suitable amount of water in the kettle and bring to boil. Slice the lemon into the thin rings and place it on the fruit plate.
- Prepare one tea bag and a suitable amount of sugar cubes.

Brewing

1 Tea set

↑ Arrange the tea set for brewing.

2 Adding water

↑ Fill the teacup with heated water until it is 7/10 full.

3 Adding tea bag

↑ Slowly lower the tea bag into the teacup, leaving the tag out of the cup.

4 Adding lemon

↑ Add the lemon ring to the tea.

5 Adding sugar

↑ Add 1 to 2 cubes of sugar and gently stir with the spoon.

★ Tea Tips ★

Use the tea bag only once. Discard after use.
After adding sugar, remember to gently stir the tea until the sugar dissolves.

Offering tea

→ Place the tea on a tray and offer it to the guests when it is ready.

More Black Tea Information

- Add the lemon according to the size of the cup. Add only a thin slice, or it will increase the bitterness of the tea. Wrap the remaining lemon in cling film and refrigerate.
- After adding lemon, the color of the tea will turn lighter and become orangey-red.
- You may add other fruits such as orange or pineapples for a variety of flavors.

Flavored Black Tea:
Coffee Black Tea

Pre-brewing Preparation

- Prepare the tea set: Kettle, teacup and saucer, tea towel, spoon, milk cup and saucer, strainer and fruit plate. Warm the coffee cup and teacup.
- Pour suitable amount of water in the kettle and bring to boil.
- Scoop suitable amount of broken black tea into the strainer. Brew the coffee and pour it into the milk cup, ready for use. Place the sugar cubes and non-dairy creamer on the fruit plate.
- Add tea leaves only up to half of the depth of the strainer. Tea leaves expand in water and might overflow into the teacup.

Brewing

1 Brewing the black tea

↑ Hold the strainer in the teacup and slowly add water.

2 Adding coffee

↑ Add the freshly brewed coffee.

3 Adding the non-dairy creamer

↑ Add 1 to 2 spoons of non-dairy creamer.

↑ Gently stir to blend.

Offering tea

→ When the Coffee Black Tea is ready, add sugar cubes according to preference.

More Black Tea Information

- *The most unique characteristic of black tea is its versatility. You can make into a variety of unique-flavored beverages by simply adding different elements.*
- *Add tea leaves only up to half of the depth of the strainer. Tea leaves expand in water and might overflow into the teacup.*

English High Tea

The early 17th century saw the export of tea from southeast China to Europe via both land and sea. The credit for this belongs to Holland. All European countries, except Russia and Portugal, bought their Chinese tea leaves from Holland. When England first imported tea leaves, it was sold in apothecaries as a form of medicine. In the 1760s, during the time of King Charles II, it slowly became a form of drink. The British queen, Portuguese princess Catherine, brought the Portuguese custom of drinking tea into the British royal family. She held tea parties that became important social functions among the aristocracy. Tea drinking in society first appeared in coffeehouses. These coffeehouses were exclusively for men; single ladies were not allowed access. The first British teahouse opened in the 19th century and became a social ground for single ladies.

Tea drinking slowly spread to all levels of the English society. The choice of tea also slowly changed from green tea to black tea. The reason that the British chose black tea over green tea was not a coincidence. Green tea does not preserve well so was not conducive for long-distance shipping. Black tea however, lasts longer. In addition, England's climate is cold and humid. There is rarely a sunny day and the skies are always gray. Such a climate is suitable for drinking black tea, which is warming. Moreover, Britishers have the habit of adding milk and sugar to tea, adding to the warmth-generating nature of the tea. Therefore, they naturally favor black tea.

The English drink tea at all times. They habitually drink tea before breakfast. During their afternoon break, they enjoy "afternoon tea." They are known for their high teas. Around 4 p.m. to 5 p.m., no matter how busy, the English drop everything, for high tea. This is a leisurely time with friends. The English prefer to add sugar, milk or lemon juice to their tea. Earl Grey Tea, Rose Tea, Peppermint Tea, Lavender tea are all favorites among the English. Over three hundred years, all the monarchs of England have remained loyal in their love for tea. They are steadfast advocates of tea drinking and believe that drinking tea is a reflection of one's elegance and charisma. England is one of the countries that imports the most tea. Its tea-drinking custom remains popular even after several hundred years.

Magical "Chilled Cream" Iced Lemon Tea

Pre-brewing Preparation

- Prepare the tea set: Kettle, a glass bottle that can withstand high temperatures, strainer, tea plate, spoon, ice cubes and fruit plate
- Pour suitable amount of water in the kettle and bring to boil.
- Slice fresh lemon and place it on the fruit plate, prepare ice cubes and some sugar cubes.
- Scoop the broken black tea onto the tea plate.

Brewing

1 Adding ice

↑ Drop the ice cubes in the glass bottle.

2 Adding lemon

↑ Place the lemon slices on top of the ice cubes.

3 Adding tea leaves

↑ Place the strainer on mouth of the bottle, and scoop the broken black tea leaves into the strainer.

4 Adding water

↑ Pour the heated water. The drink will be ready in 3 to 5 minutes.

↑ Add a little sugar. The creamy texture of the drink is the reason it is known as "Chilled Cream Tea."

Refreshing Iced Peppermint Tea

Brewing

★ Tea Tips ★

Other than peppermint powder, you may add diced dried fruits to black tea to make fruit tea.

1 Tea set

↑ Prepare a clean ice cube tray, peppermint powder and brewed black tea.

2 Adding peppermint

↑ Distribute the peppermint powder evenly into the ice cube tray.

3 Adding the tea liquid

← Pour the brewed black tea into the ice cube tray, cover it properly and freeze it. When drinking tea, simply add a black tea ice cube into the fresh black tea. It will not dilute the taste of the black tea, instead add a refreshing mint taste.

★ Tea Tips ★

Other flavors of iced tea, such as iced Oolong tea or iced green tea can also be brewed in the same method. Instead of peppermint you may use sugar to make a sweeter drink.

Use the same method to make green tea ice cubes, Oolong tea ice cubes, Pu-erh tea ice cubes that can be added into different teas for extra flavor.

Column 3

Tea Wares

Tea wares are the items used to brew tea. The same type of tea brewed with the same method but with tea sets of different material and quality will result in teas of a different color, fragrance and taste. The methods of brewing tea keep changing. Similarly, the tea sets also vary. Today, there are many varieties of tea sets for the tea brewer to choose from.

Classification of Tea Sets

Ceramic tea sets

The best type of ceramic tea set is the Yixing Zisha tea set. Usually Zisha tea sets are not glazed. The most frequently seen item in the Zisha tea set is the Zisha teapot. One of the merits of brewing in a Zisha teapot is that the tea will not lose its original flavor. It is heat resistant and can also be used to simmer tea. It does not scald the hand. It is durable. After prolonged use, even water poured from it will be tea-scented. The teapot exterior instead of becoming dull acquires sheen. Therefore it is a favorite among collectors. Other than the teapot, there are also other Zisha-made items of the tea set such as the Zisha teacup, Zisha double-layered tea tray, Zisha basic, etc.

Porcelain tea set

The porcelain tea set has always been popular. All items used in brewing tea such as the tea bowl, the teapot, the fairness cup, the aroma cup, etc., come in all shapes and colors in porcelain. Color-wise, there are white, green and black porcelain tea sets. In addition, there are other alternative variations of glazed porcelain, famille-rose porcelain, doucai porcelain, blue-white porcelain, etc.

Bamboo and wooden tea sets

Bamboo and wooden tea sets are both economical and practical. They have a rustic charm of their own. They are also flexible in terms of decoration. Well-carved bamboo or wooden tea sets are collectors' items. Frequently seen items are the tea tray, the tea plate and the six helpers in the art of tea.

Glass tea sets

The characteristic of glass tea sets is in its transparency, enabling the tea drinker to admire the "dance of tea leaves" as well as the color of the tea liquid. Using glass to boil water helps estimate the temperature of the water. It is risky to handle. Frequently seen items include the teapot, the fairness cup, the tea appreciation cup and the kettle.

Stainless steel tea set

The kettle is usually made of stainless steel. It is a quick conductor of heat and nonporous.

Other types of tea sets

Other types of tea sets, usually more ornamental than useful, include lacquered tea sets, cloisonné tea sets, stone tea sets, jade tea sets, china tea sets, etc.

Choosing a Tea Set

The choice of the tea set depends on the type of tea leaves and the number of people drinking the tea. First, decide whether to brew in a cup or in the pot. Then choose according to the number of guests. The items in the tea set should match. Some supporting items can be used ingeniously, such as a bowl as the water basin.

A Basic Tea Set for a Master Tea Brewer

- A kettle for boiling water
- Main tea brewing wares: Teapot (Zisha teapot, porcelain teapots, etc.), tea bowl, teacup (both big glass teacups and small tea appreciation cups), fairness cup.
- Supporting tea wares: Tea plate, aroma cup, tea saucer, tea jar, the six helpers (tea scoop, teaspoon, tea pick, tea tongs, tea funnel, Yanghu brush), double-layered tea tray, strainer, strainer stand, basin and tea towel.

Spirited Allure: Oolong Tea

The appreciation of Oolong t
focuses on its special allu
known in Chinese as "Yu
meaning "the allure of Oolo
tea." Different Oolong teas ha
their own unique allure.

Oolong Tea Producti

Freshly picked leaves

↓

Withering

↓

Partial drying

↓

Rolling and shaping

↓

Drying

Basic Oolong Tea Knowledge

Water temperature	Should be above 95°
Ratio of leaves to water	1:22
Appropriate tea sets	Include Zisha and porcelain tea sets
Steeping time	First short then long

Oolong Tea Facts

- When brewing Oolong tea, the water temperature should be very high. Water that has just reached boiling point is the most suitable.
- Oolong tea leaves must be moisturized before brewing. The water used to moisturize the tea leaves should be quickly drained.
- When pouring water for brewing, top up the teapot.
- For tea leaves that are tightly wound into a ball, such as Tieguanyin, Gold Cassia or Dongding Wulong, fill 1/4 or 1/3 of the teapot. For tea leaves that are twisted into strips, such as Dahongpao or Fenghuang Dancong, fill about 2/3 or 4/5 of the teapot. The tea leaves should not overflow after expanding upon absorbing moisture. If you cannot replace the lid properly, it means that too much tea leaves were added. This is not only a waste, it will also affect the flavor of the tea.
- The steeping time for each round of tea is approximately 30–40 seconds and it is increases with additional rounds. Different types of tea leaves of varying quality (production place and harvested season) will have varying steeping time.

"Yin Yun" Tieguanyin

Pre-brewing Preparation

- Prepare the tea set: Kettle, tea plate, double-layered tea tray, small traveling set tea bowl, tea appreciation cup, teaspoon and tea towel.
- Pour suitable amount of water in the kettle and bring to boil.
- Gently scoop the Tieguanyin tea leaves onto the tea plate.

Brewing

★ Tea Tips ★

After adding the tea leaves, cover the tea bowl. Shake it gently before taking off the lid to inhale the scent of dried tea leaves.

The traveling tea set is small and convenient. It is a good choice for brewing Gongfu tea in the countryside.

1 Tea set

← Arrange the tea set for brewing.

2 Warming the tea set

↑ Use the tea bowl instead of the teapot. Add heated water to warm the tea bowl.

↑ Next, pour the water into the tea appreciation cup to warm the tea appreciation cup.

3 Adding tea leaves

↑ Spoon the tea leaves into the tea bowl.

↑ Add approximately 6-8gms of Tieguanyin tea leaves into the tea bowl.

4 Moisturizing tea

↑ Pour heated water into the tea bowl and immediately pour it into the tea appreciation cup.

5 Formal brewing

↑ Fill the tea bowl to the brim with heated water.

6 Removing the foam

↑ Use the lid to remove the foam from the rim of the tea bowl.

↑ Rinse the lid with the heated water and cover the tea bowl.

7 Warming tea appreciation cup

↑ Dip the cup into the first round of tea liquid one by one to warm the cup. Pour the water in the last cup into the tea tray.

8 Distributing tea

↑ Distribute the tea into the lined teacups in a smooth sweeping arc. This is known as "General Guan touring the city walls." This evenly distributes the flavor of the tea.

↑ Distribute the essence of the tea equally in each cup, a single drop per cup. This is known as "Han Xin inspecting the troops."

Offering tea

← Offer the freshly brewed tea with both hands to the guests.

More Oolong Tea Information

- Using the tea bowl to brew Tieguanyin is both convenient and easy. However, porcelain is a quick heat conductor, thus the tea bowl scalds the hand easily. Amateurs should use Zisha Teapot to brew tea.
- When using the tea bowl to brew tea, inhale the aroma of the tea from the tea lid.
- Tieguanyin is good for brewing 3–5 rounds.
- Tieguanyin tea leaves are whorl-shaped and heavy. The color is dark green and the aroma is fresh and long-lasting. It has a natural orchid scent. The color of the tea liquid is gold and clear, the taste is rich, mellow and sweet. The allure "Yin Yun" is defined. The tea leaves are thick and well-shaped. The color of the leaves is green edged with red.

"Yan Yun" Dahongpao

Pre-brewing Preparation

- Prepare the tea set: Clay alcohol burner, clay kettle, basin, Zisha teapot, fairness cup, tea plate, tea towel, tea appreciation cup and saucer and teapot holder.
- Fill the clay kettle with water, light the alcohol burner and bring to boil.
- Scoop the Dahongpao tea leaves onto the tea plate.

Brewing

1 Tea set

↑ Arrange the tea set for brewing.

★ Tea Tips ★

Dahongpao tea leaves are shaped like small rolls and thus take up more space. Add leaves up to 2/3 to 4/5 of the teapot space.

2 Warming the tea set

↑ Pour the boiling water into the Zisha teapot.

↑ Pour the water from the Zisha teapot into the fairness cup.

↑ Pour the water from the fairness cup into the tea appreciation cup.

3 Adding tea leaves

↑ Replace the teapot lid with the tea funnel.

↑ Use a teaspoon to add the tea leaves into the teapot.

↑ Replace lid again.

4 Moisturizing tea

↑ Fill half the teapot with water and quickly pour it into the fairness cup.

5 Formal brewing

↑ Fill the teapot to the brim.

6 Removing the foam

↑ Use the lid of the teapot to remove the foam at the rim and cover the teapot.

7 Sealing the tea

↑ Use the water in the fairness cup to rinse the teapot to seal the flavor of the tea.

8 Warming the teacup

↑ Drain the water from the teacup into the basin.

↑ Dry the exterior of the teacup before replacing it on the saucer.

9 Readying the brew

↑ After sealing the tea for about 30 seconds, uncover the lid of the fairness cup and pour the freshly brewed tea into the fairness cup.

10 Distributing tea

← Distribute the tea evenly from the fairness cup into each individual tea appreciation cup.

Offering tea

↑ Offer the tea to the guests with both hands.

- If the fairness cup has a strainer, there is no need to use a strainer.
- Method of handling the overhead handle teapot:

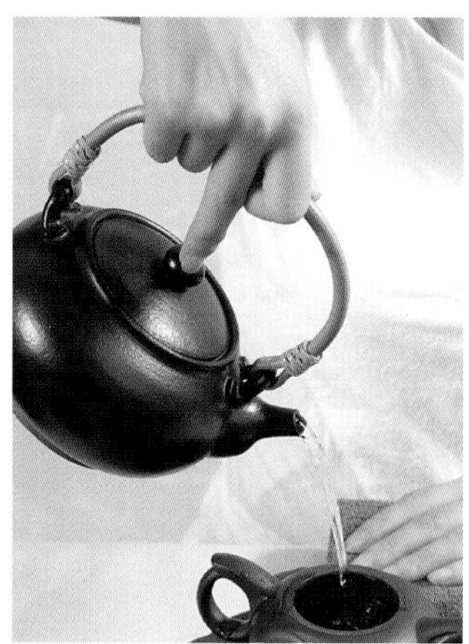

↑ Single hand – Press the teapot lid with the third finger while wrapping the other fingers around the handle.

More Oolong Tea Information

- Dahongpao can be brewed for 6–8 rounds.
- Dahongpao is known as a treasure among teas. The tea leaves are balanced and compact, the color dark green and shiny. The color of the tea is a bright golden orange with a natural floral scent. The taste is refreshing, rich and very sweet.The "Yan Yun" –rock allure is defined. The leaves are soft and glossy, green edged with red.
- You may use the single-hand method of lifting the teapot.
- You may use two hands to lift the teapot.

↑ Two hands – Hold the handle with one hand while pressing the the teapot lid with the third finger of the other hand.

"Qing Yun" Dongding Oolong

Pre-brewing Preparation

- Prepare the tea set: Kettle, double-layered tea tray, six helpers in the art of tea, Zisha teapot, fairness cup, strainer and stand, tea plate, tea towel, aroma plate, tea appreciation cup and saucer.
- Fill the kettle with water and bring to boil.
- Scoop the Dongding Oolong tea leaves onto the tea plate.

Brewing

1 Tea set

← Arrange the tea set for brewing.

★ Tea Tips ★

Fill approximately 1/4 of the teapot with Dongding Oolong tea leaves.

2 Warming the tea set

↑ Fill the teapot with heated water.

↑ Warm the fairness cup.

↑ Warm the aroma cup and the tea appreciation cup.

3 Adding tea leaves

↑ Replace the lid of the teapot with the tea funnel.

↑ Gently add the Dongding Oolong tea leaves into the teapot with the teaspoon.

4 Moisturizing tea leaves

↑ Fill half the teapot with water and quickly pour it into the fairness cup.

5 Formal brewing

↑ Fill the teapot to the brim.

6 Removing the foam

↑ Use the lid of the teapot to remove the foam at the rim and cover the teapot.

7 Sealing the tea

→ Use the water in the fairness cup to rinse the teapot to seal the flavor of the tea.

8 Warming the teacup

↑ Use tea tongs to warm the tea appreciation cup. Pouring the water into the aroma cup.

↑ Pick up the tea towel with the left hand to dry the tea appreciation cup.

↑ Drain the water from the aroma cup into the tea tray.

↑ Use the tea towel to dry the aroma cup before replacing it.

9 Readying the brew

↑ After sealing the teapot for approximately 30 seconds, pour the tea into the fairness cup.

↑ Try your best to empty the teapot.

10 Distributing tea

→ Evenly distribute the tea from the fairness cup into each individual aroma cup.

Offering tea

> **★ Tea Tips ★**
> There are three ways of inhaling the aroma of the tea–inhaling from the tea appreciation cup, inhaling from the lid or tea liquid when using the tea bowl to brew tea and inhaling from the aroma cup.

← Offer the freshly brewed Dongding Oolong tea on a tea tray to the guest with both hands.

Inhaling the Aroma of the Tea

↑ Pour the tea in the aroma cup into the tea appreciation cup.

↑ Hold the aroma cup with both hands to the nose to inhale the fragrance of the Dongding Oolong.

Drinking the Tea

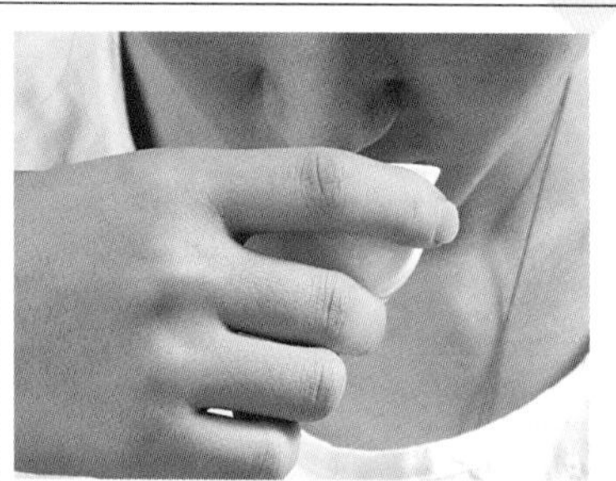

↑ Hold the tea in the "three dragons protecting the cauldron" way and slowly sip the tea.

More Oolong Tea Information

- The bright green Dongding Oolong tea leaves are tightly wound into small balls. The dried tea leaves have a strong fragrance. The liquid is bright golden with a strong floral fragrance; the taste is smooth and mellow.
- After distributing the tea into the aroma cup, cover with the tea appreciation cup. Holding firmly, quickly flip the two cups around. Serve it to the guests with both hands. When appreciating the fragrance of the tea, pick up the aroma cup and roll it between the hands before bringing it to the nose.

↑ Cover the aroma cup with the tea appreciation cup. Use the thumb to press the tea appreciation cup firmly on the aroma cup and hold the aroma cup with the second and third finger.

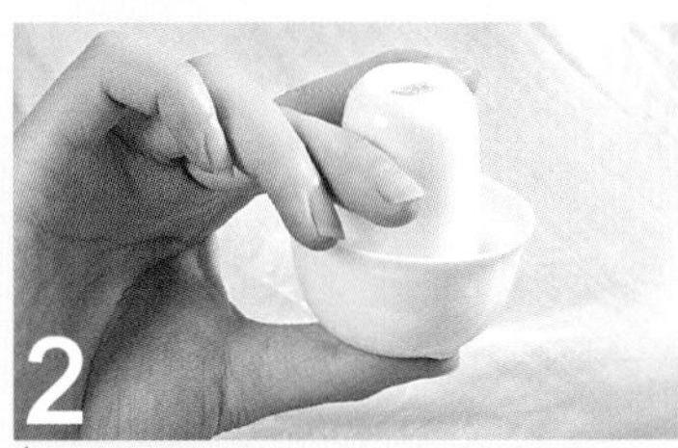

↑ Flip the two cups around. The movement must be quick but not too strong to splash the tea liquid. Ladies should keep their movements to minimal.

↑ Place the cups on the tea tray and serve it to the guests with both hands.

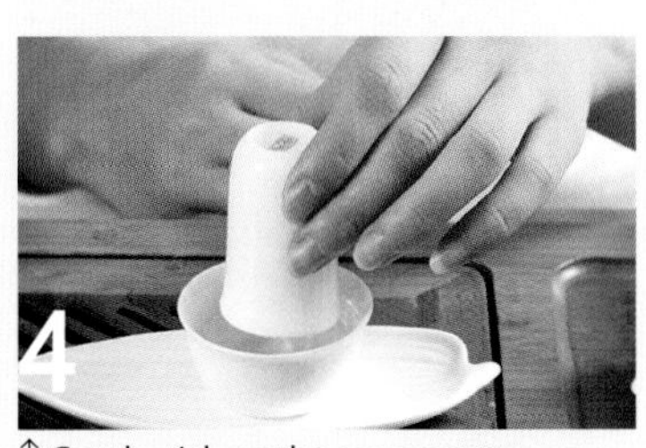

↑ Gently pick up the aroma cup.

↑ Allow the tea to flow into the tea appreciation cup.

↑ Roll the aroma cup between the hands before bringing it to the nose to breathe in the fragrance.

Column 4

Brewing and Enjoying Tea in the Countryside

The green hills, streams, a lone boat, passing clouds, spiraling smoke in the distance, the setting sun and the fragrance of tea—what more can you ask for? The tranquility of the painting *Drinking Tea with Master Yuan at Qingshan Lake* by Reverent Lingyi of the Tang Dynasty is most sought after by all tea lovers.

For the modern city dweller, it is not difficult to plan an excursion with friends to the countryside to drink tea. Wake up early on a sunny day. Pack a tea set, find a scenic spot and begin brewing tea. Catch up with your friends amid the calming backdrop of lakes and mountains. The perfect way to escape life occasionally!

Preparation

- Pay attention to the weather forecast and pick a sunny day. Check to make sure that it is not too windy.
- Pick a familiar route to avoid spending time on the road.
- Pick a place with a convenient water source, preferably near a spring or well. The water should be clean and of good quality. If the area does not have any water source, take your own container of purified or mineral water.
- Find a safe place to light a fire. Flat stony areas by the waterside are the best. Carry fuel such charcoal or alcohol to light the fire. Pick firewood or dried branches for added fuel. If you are at a place where lighting fires are not allowed, you have two options. Boil water at home and bring it along in a thermos, or find a small shop nearby and ask for heated water.
- The countryside is usually colder than the city. The wind is usually stronger too. Remember to dress accordingly.
- Wear flat shoes and comfortable clothes. If it is very sunny, remember to carry your sun block, sunglasses and hats.

Things to carry:

Fuel for boiling water: Charcoal, firewood, solid or liquid alcohol.

Water containers: Water ladle and water containers.

Tea set: Tea tray, teapot, fairness cup, tea appreciation cup and saucer, basin, tea towel, kettle and tea jar (with tea leaves).

Other equipment: Lighter or matches, trash bags, rugs, cushions, wet tissues, dry tissues, paper cups, towels, cameras, etc.

Brewing Tea

Upon reaching the destination, first find a place to settle down. After setting down the things, find water, light the fire, boil the water and set up the tea set in preparation for brewing.

Getting Water

↑ Carry a water ladle and a container. Ask the local people for the right drinking water source. As Lu Yu said in his *Classic of Tea*, spring water can be found in the valleys or under the cliffs. Groundwater that seeped through the earth is the freshest and clearest water and best for brewing tea.

Lighting the fire

↑ Follow the stones along the river until you find a slightly flat and smooth surface. Use three big stones to form a tripod and place the charcoal in the center before using the solid alcohol to light the fire.

Boiling Water

↑ Pour the spring water into the clay teapot and place it on the makeshift tripod. The most difficult step of brewing tea is boiling water. During the Tang Dynasty, people observed the air bubbles in the water to determine the temperature of the water. During the Song Dynasty, they depended on the sound of the boiling water to determine the water temperature. Since we are using a clay teapot to boil water, let us follow the Song Dynasty. As we heat the water, pay attention to the sound of the water in the teapot. When we hear the sound of the water bubbling and see the vapors steaming out from the spout, we know that the water has reached boiling point.

Brewing Tea

← Follow the steps of brewing tea. Warm the teapot, the cup, add the tea leaves, moisturize the tea, ready the brew, distribute the tea and finally appreciate the tea. Repeat the steps as needed. Take your time, and do not rush. If the water is good and the mood is good, the tea will naturally be the best you've tasted.

Clearing up

Before leaving, check and make sure that everything is properly stowed. Clear everything up. Ensure that you leave no trash, only your footprints. That'll be the perfect ending to a beautiful day.

More tips on brewing tea in the countryside

- When boiling water, remember to add water into the clay teapot in time, or else the clay teapot will crack.
- If the wind is strong, remember to check the fire. Place the tea set away from the wind. It might blow ashes into the teacups or tea pot.
- Have your tea with small snacks, but do not eat facing the wind.
- Place the tea set in a stable position. Be gentle when handling the delicate tea sets as they crack easily.
- Remember to douse the fire properly to prevent accident. Use the leftover water in the basin to douse the cinders well.
- The stones that supported the kettle will be extremely hot; don't touch them.
- Clean the tea set with the remaining heated water before drying with the towel. Then wrap them up properly with paper.
- Do not leave the trash. Pack them in the trash bags and dispose at home.

Fascinating Pu-erh

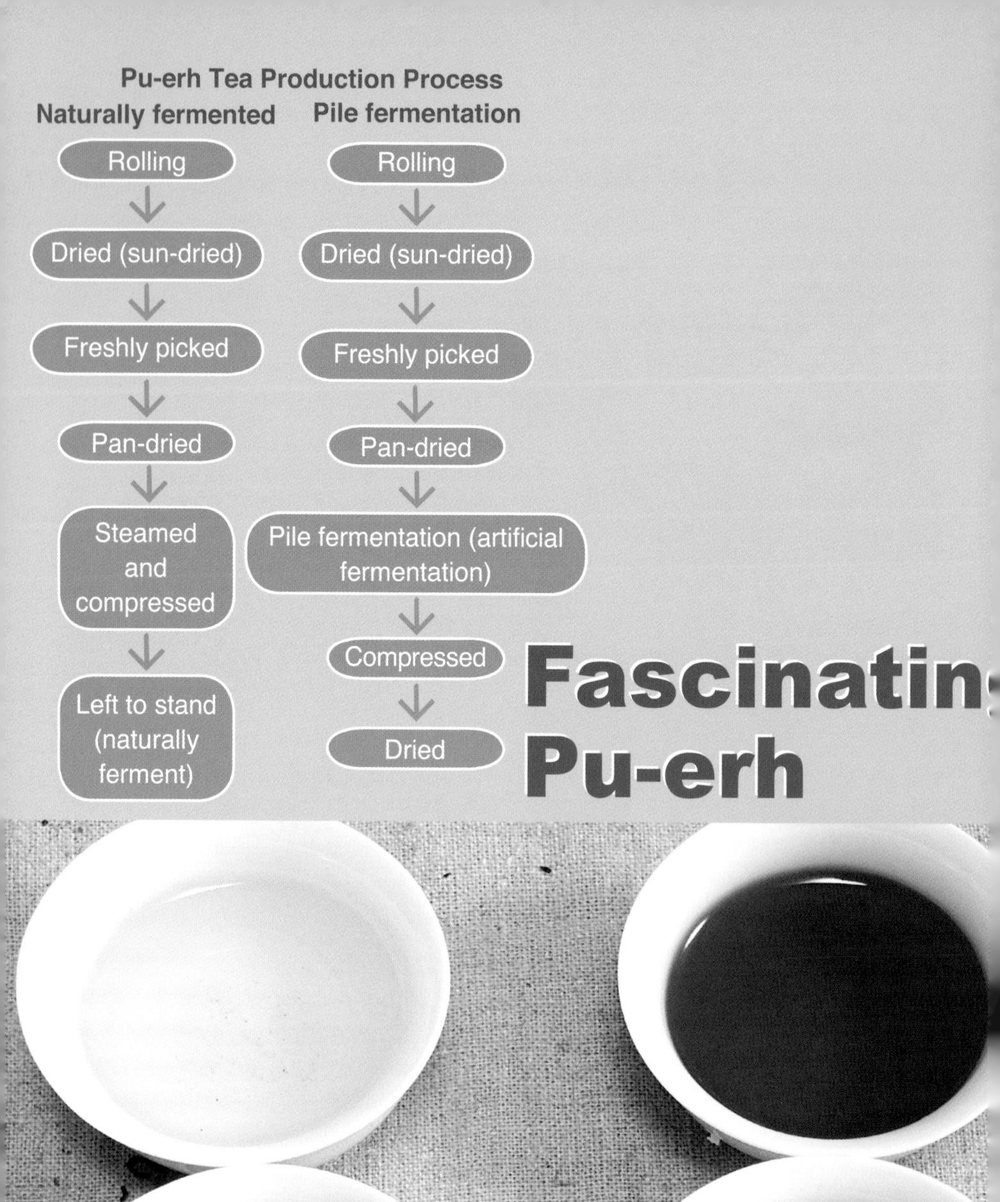

Basic Pu-erh Tea Knowledge

Water temperature	Should be 100°
Tea leaves to water ratio	1:50 or 1:30
Appropriate tea sets	Include Zisha teapot and tea bowl and tea appreciation cups made of white porcelain or glass.

Pu-erh Tea Facts

- Moisturize the Pu-erh tea leaves before brewing. The first round of boiling water that is poured into the teapot must be drained immediately. If necessary, repeat this step once or twice more.
- The brewing time should be first short then long. The first round after moisturizing the tea leaves should be between 30 to 60 seconds. Then pour the tea into the fairness cup. The brewing time is usually adjusted in accordance to the age and quality of the tea leaves.
- Pu-erh tea can usually be brewed up to 8 rounds and above.
- Use the tea knife to break off the tea leaves from compressed tea.

Pu-erh Tea refers to tea produced in the ancient Pu-erh Prefecture (currently Yunnan Xishuangbanna and Simao areas). Pu-erh tea is made with the large-leaf sun-dried "mao" tea leaves of this area. After fermentation, they are made into loose or compressed tea.

Rising Fragrance:
Green Pu-erh Tea

Pre-brewing Preparation

- Preparing the tea set: Kettle, tea knife, green Pu-erh tea, teapot, fairness cup, strainer, tea appreciation cup, tea plate, tea towel, double-layered tea tray and tea coaster.
- Fill the kettle with water and bring to boil.
- Use the tea knife to break away the tea leaves and place them on the tea plate.

Brewing

1 Tea set

← Arrange the tea set to brew the tea.

★ Tea Tips ★

- Use your hands to loosen the tea leaves before brewing.

2 Warming the tea set

↑ Pour heated water into the teapot.

↑ Pour the water into the fairness cup.

↑ Pour the water into the tea appreciation cup.

3 Adding tea leaves

← Use the tea knife to break off the tea leaves from the compressed tea onto the tea plate. Then gently sweep the tea leaves from the tea plate into the teapot.

4 Moisturizing tea

↑ Fill half the teapot with water.

↑ Quickly drain it into the tea tray. Repeat 1–3 times.

5 Brewing the tea

↑ Fill the teapot.

↑ Remove the foam with the lid of the teapot, brew for approximately 30 seconds.

6 Warming the teacup

↑ Warming the teacup – see pg. 23.

↑ Drain the water used to warm the teacup into the tea tray.

7 Readying the brew

↑ Pour the freshly brewed tea into the fairness cup.

↑ Try your best to empty the teapot.

8 Distributing tea

↑ Hold the fairness cup with one hand and the tea towel with the other.

↑ Dry the spout of the fairness cup each time after filling a cup of tea.

Offering tea

↑ Place the tea appreciation cup on the saucer and serve it with both hands to the guests.

More Pu-erh Tea Information

- One- to two-year old Green Pu-erh Tea's color is similar to green tea. With a slightly bitter taste, it has a strong fragrance, which lingers in the teacup even after the tea is over.
- The fragrance of Green Pu-erh is overpowering. Green Pu-erh may be too strong for some stomachs. Therefore, note the reactions of your body when drinking Green Pu-erh tea.

Aged Fragrance:
Cooked Pu-erh Tea

Pre-brewing Preparation

- Preparing the tea set: Kettle, Zisha teapot, fairness cup, tea knife, cooked Pu-erh tea, strainer, double-layered tea appreciation cup, tea plate, tea towel, double-layered tea tray and tea coaster.
- Fill the kettle with water and bring to boil.
- Use the tea knife to break away the tea leaves and place them on the tea plate.

Brewing

1 Tea set

← Arrange the tea set to brew the tea.

★ Tea Tips ★

- Whether it's Green Pu-erh or Cooked Pu-erh, both have a long fermentation period. Therefore, don't skip the moisturizing process. If necessary, moisturize the tea two or three times. The water used must be boiling hot and should be drained away immediately.

2 Warming the tea set

↑ Pour heated water into the teapot.

↑ Pour the water into the fairness cup.

↑ Pour the water into the tea appreciation cup.

3 Adding tea leaves

← Add the Pu-erh tea leaves into the teapot.

4 Moisturizing tea leaves

↑ Pour boiling water into the teapot.

↑ Pour water from the teapot into the fairness cup.

5 Brewing

↑ Fill the teapot with water.

↑ Remove the foam with the lid before covering the teapot.

6 Sealing the teapot

→ Pour the water in the fairness cup over the teapot to seal the flavor of the tea, and let it stand for about 1 minute.

7 Warming the teacup

↑ See Pg 23 for the steps to warm the teacup.

↑ Drain the water in the teacup into the tea tray.

8 Readying the brew

↑ Pour the freshly brewed tea into the fairness cup, try your best to empty the teapot.

9 Distributing tea

↑ Hold the fairness cup with one hand and the tea towel with the other. Evenly distribute the tea in the fairness cup into each individual tea appreciation cup.

Offering tea

↑ Serve the tea with both hands to the guests.

★ Tea Tips ★

- Use a double-layered glass tea appreciation cup to protect the hand from being scalded when picking up the cup. It is aesthetically pleasing and also keeps the tea warm. However, remember to lower the head slightly when drinking and avoid tilting the cup too much or the tea might overflow.

Some Pu-erh Tea Information

- Both Cooked and Green Pu-erh teas are stored for a period of time to allow natural fermentation before being subjected to pile fermentation.
- Cooked Pu-erh tea is fully fermented. Therefore it has a smoother and warmer taste. Amateur Pu-erh tea drinkers are advised to start with Cooked Pu-erh tea.

In the Mood for Pu-erh: Mixed Green and Cooked Pu-erh

Pre-brewing Preparation

Pour both brewed sun-dried Pu-erh and Cooked Pu-erh into the fairness cup and tea appreciation cup to warm.

Brewing

1 Distributing Green Pu-erh tea liquid

← Line six cups in a straight row and fill each cup according to the following: 6/10 full, 5/10 full, 4/10 full, 3/10 full, 2/10 full and 1/10 full.

★ Tea Tips ★

● You can switch the order and first pour the Cooked Pu-erh tea before adding the equivalent amount of Green Pu-erh tea.

2 Distributing Cooked Pu-erh tea liquid

↑ Fill each cup 7/10 full with the cooked tea liquid.

3 Appreciating the tea

↑ Choose the tea that suits your taste to drink and appreciate.

More Pu-erh Tea Information

- Even under suitable climate, naturally fermented Pu-erh tea leaves take a number of years to fully ferment. Tea that has been stored for different span of years varies in terms of the color of the tea leaves, the color of the tea liquor and taste.
- Mixing the brew of green Pu-erh and cooked Pu-erh in different stages of fermentation give varying tastes. Naturally, this brewing art takes a lot of time and patience to practice.

OVERWHELMING FRAGRANCE:
Brewing Pu-erh Tea

Pre-brewing Preparation

- Preparing the tea set: Kettle, tea plate, glass teacup, teaspoon, basin, tea towel and glass teapot.
- Fill the kettle with water and bring to boil.
- Scoop a suitable amount of loose Pu-erh tea (cooked) onto the tea plate.

Brewing

1 Preparing the tea set

↑ Arrange the tea set for brewing.

2 Warming the tea set

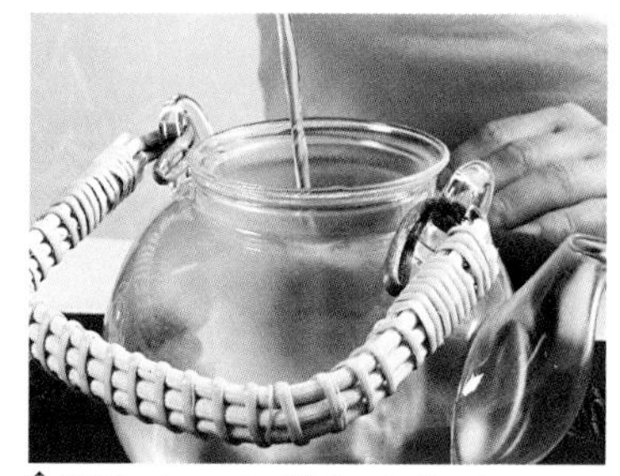

↑ Fill the teapot with heated water.

↑ Pour the water from the teapot into the teacup.

3 Adding tea leaves

↑ Gently scoop the tea leaves into the teapot.

4 Moisturizing tea leaves

↑ Pour a small amount of heated water into the teapot.

↑ Drain the water in the teapot into the basin.

5 Brewing

↑ Add boiling water.

↑ Simmer in the teapot for 2 to 3 minutes.

5 Warming the teacup

↑ Pour the water in the teacup and then drain into the basin.

↑ Dry the teacup with the tea towel before replacing it on the saucer.

7 Distributing tea

↑ Distribute the tea into the teacups.

More Pu-erh Tea Information

- Simmering will make the flavor of Pu-erh tea even stronger, the scent heady and overwhelming. If you are not used to drinking such strongly flavored tea, but enjoy hot tea, reduce the amount of tea leaves.

Mellowed Fragrance: Pu-erh Milk Tea

Pre-brewing Preparation

- Prepare freshly brewed tea.
- Heat the milk.

Brewing

> **★ Tea Tips ★**
> - Choose a stainless steel, porcelain or glass kettle that can withstand high temperatures.
> - Glass kettles are aesthetically pleasing but very delicate. Therefore, handle them with care.

1 Pouring Tea

← Pour the brewed tea into the teacup.

2 Adding milk

↑ Add heated milk into the cup.

3 Drinking

↑ Stir well with a spoon.

More Pu-erh Tea Information

- Adjust the ratio of tea to milk according to personal preference.
- Add salt or sugar for a more unique flavor.
- Use Cooked Pu-erh tea when mixing flavored Pu-erh tea.

Column 5

The Story of Pu-erh

Pu-erh tea is a fascinating multifaceted tea. Its unique history originates from the horseback. For a thousand years, Pu-Erh tea traveled from Pu-erh Prefecture to exotic places such as Tibet, Vietnam, Laos and Myanmar. Legends spread about this intriguing tea together with the stories of the Horse Gang and the ancient Tea-horse route.

Pu-erh Prefecture Pu-erh Tea

Pu-erh Prefecture was first established during the reign of Emperor Yongzheng (Qing Dynasty). The area includes the current Simao, Xishuangbanna and Linchang. Pu-erh Prefecture was the main distribution center for all the tea leaves produced in Diannan. It was exported to other areas by the Horse Gang through the ancient Tea-horse route. Pu-erh tea was named after Pu-erh Prefecture.

Produced in the areas of Simao, Xishuangbanna, Pu-erh tea is made from the large Yunnan tea leaves that are sun-dried before being steamed and compressed into tea disks or tea bricks. It is later placed in a cool and dry area to dry naturally. Every seven disks are packaged into one tube known as "Qizi Tea Disk," tied with husk rope. These tea disks are marketed in Tibet. The long and difficult journey from Pu-erh Prefecture to Lhasa with varying climate changes causes the tea disk to continuously ferment, resulting in the unique scent of the Pu-erh tea much favored by the Tibetans.

Ancient Tea-horse Route and the Pu-erh Tea

Pu-erh tea became internationally renowned since the Ming and Qing dynasties.

Five famous Tea-horse routes are centered around Pu-erh:

- The official route: Connecting Pu-erh to Kunning and later to the mainland provinces.
- Diancang Tea-horse route: Connecting Pu-erh to Tibet through Jinggu, Jingdong, Nanjian, Xiaguan, Lijiang, Zhongdian (the current Shangri-la).
- Jianglai Tea-horse route: Connecting Pu-erh to Vietnam's Laizhou through Jiancheng.
- Drought season Tea-horse route: Connecting Pu-erh to Myanmar through Lancang and Menglian.
- Mengla Tea-horse route: Connecting Pu-erh to Laos through Mengla.
- With the growth of New China, transportation in the Yunnan province developed rapidly. Carriages replaced horses. Later, cars and trains replaced carriages and the horses slowly disappeared.
- Mengla Tea-horse route: Connecting Pu-erh to Laos through Mengla. With the growth of New China, transportation in the Yunnan province

developed rapidly. Carriages replaced horses. Later, cars and trains replaced carriages and the horses slowly disappeared from the Tea-horse routes.

The Versatile Pu-erh Tea

From the 1930s, improvement in the modes of transportation drastically reduced travel time from Pu-erh to Tibet. This naturally affected the natural fermentation process of the Pu-erh tea. Therefore, in the 1970s, artificially fermented or cooked Pu-erh tea, also known as "Shou Pu," appeared in the market. Cooked Pu-erh tea's quick fermentation process still uses the large-leafed sun-dried green tea. The sun-dried tea leaves undergo a unique process known as "pile fermentation." The tea leaves are first splashed with water, then piled evenly before being covered with a damp hemp cloth and allowed to ferment. After a certain period, the tea leaves slowly turn reddish-brown. The tea leaves are spread out to dry naturally. Thereafter, they are separated according to quality either into Pu-erh loose tea or compressed tea.

Traditional Production and Modern Production

Traditonal Pu-erh tea refers to the naturally fermented Pu-erh tea, also known as "Old Tea." This type of tea uses the Yunnan large-leafed sun-dried "mao" tea leaves that are stored and compressed into various forms of compressed tea. It is stored for periods ranging from a few years to ten or twenty years or more. This forms the unique smooth, sweet, rich and mellow Pu-erh flavor. Modern Pu-erh refers to the artificially fermented Pu-erh tea (cooked tea or "Shou Pu"). The aroma of age is achieved through the repeated steps of splashing water and piling.

"Dry Storage" Pu-erh Tea

Pu-erh tea that is stored in a cool storehouse and allowed to age slowly is known as "dry storage" Pu-erh tea.

"Wet Storage" Pu-erh Tea

Dry compressed tea or processed Pu-erh tea that is placed in a humid storehouse will ferment quickly. Some places store sun-dried "mao" tea in a humid storehouse before compressing. The tea's characteristic is its aged color and obvious "wet storage" flavor.

Storing Pu-erh Tea

The key factors that affect the quality of the tea leaves are humidity, temperature, oxygen and light. Typically, a good place to store Pu-erh tea should be well ventilated, dry, dark, unscented and hygienic. You can store a small amount of Pu-erh tea in your home. It is best to choose compressed tea as this comes in small sizes and preserves well. Unwrap the compressed tea and store it in a clean jar or simply wrap it in a porous paper and let it age naturally. You will be able to enjoy the unique aged scent after few years. Naturally fermented Pu-erh tea (also known as Green Pu-erh tea) can keep for more than 10 years. Artificially fermented Pu-erh tea (Cooked Pu-erh tea) can keep for a couple of years. Whether the Pu-erh tea is fermented naturally or not, there is an optimal number of years of fermentation. Continued fermenting will cause the quality to decline. Therefore, once the Pu-erh tea has reached its peak in terms of color, fragrance, taste and spirit, do not keep it any longer.

Appreciating Pu-erh Tea

Top-grade Pu-erh tea is not only a wonderful drink, it is also worth collecting. Quality Pu-erh tea is made from quality tea leaves. The tea leaves have to be the perfectly shaped Yunnan arbor-shaped large leaf. The color should be shining brown. Compressed tea must also be perfectly shaped and balanced. Even after many rounds of brewing, if the color, fragrance and taste do not change much, the tea liquid remains a clear bright red, the fragrance pure and clear and the taste still smooth, sweet and rich, then this is good quality Pu-erh tea.

Elegance in Tea: Yellow Tea

Yellow Tea Production Process

Rolling and shaping

↓

Simmering

↓

Freshly picked leaves

↓

Pan-drying

↓

Drying

Yellow Tea is relatively unknown to most people. It is indeed rarely seen. Some books classify Yellow Tea as part of the Green Tea family. It is rare to find Yellow Tea even in teahouses.

Basic Yellow Tea Knowledge

Water Temperature	Approximately 80°
Appropriate tea sets	Glass or porcelain teacup (teapot)
Ratio of tea leaves to water	1:50

Yellow Tea Facts

- Yellow tea and green tea have similar characteristics, therefore use the same green tea brewing method.
- When brewing yellow bud tea such as Huoshan Yellow bud tea, Mengting Yellow bud tea, the water temperature should be maintained at approximately 80°. However, Junshan Silver Needles is an exception. The tea buds are thick and hairy. If the water temperature is too low, it will be difficult for the tea bud to absorb water. If necessary, one should even cover the teacup with an extra layer of glass in order to cause the tea bud to begin "dancing" to absorb water in five minutes. The "dance of tea leaves" of the Junshan Silver Needles is one of the best among tea leaves dances. It has a unique "three rises and three falls" pattern.

Dance of the Leaves:
Junshan Silver Needles

Pre-brewing Preparation

- Preparing the tea set: Kettle, glass tea cup, basin, tea towel, teaspoon, saucer and tea plate.
- Fill the kettle with water and bring to boil. Allow the temperature to drop to 85° before use.
- Gently scoop a suitable amount of Junshan Silver Needles tea leaves onto the tea plate.

Brewing

1 Tea set

← Arrange the tea set for brewing.

2 Warming the cup

↑ Warm the cup and drain the water into the basin.

3 Adding the water

↑ Fill 1/3 of the cup with heated water.

4 Adding tea leaves

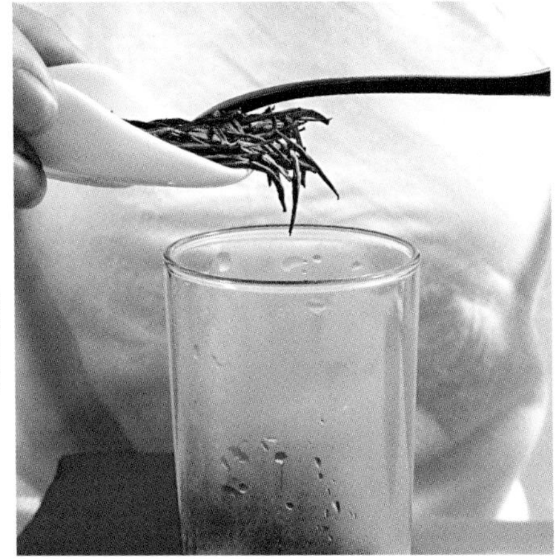

↑ Gently scoop the Junshan Silver Needles tea leaves into the glass teacup.

5 Adding water again

↑ Fill the teacup until it is 7/10 full. Hold the kettle at a height when pouring the water so that the force of the water will scatter the tea leaves apart.

★ Tea Tips ★

Junshan Silver Needles are most pleasing to brew. Take the time to admire the crystal bubbles and dancing tea leaves in the glass teacup. The tea will be ready after approximately 5 minutes.

Offering tea

↑ Offer the tea to the guests with both hands.

Admiring the dance of the tea leaves

↑ Silently admire the tea leaves dance.

More Yellow Tea Information

- Junshan Silver Needles tea leaves will not float to the top of the cup immediately upon coming in contact with water. It will take 3 to 5 minutes to fully absorb the water, the tip of the tea bud will face up and it will float up and down for a while before slowly sinking to the bottom of the cup. Some tea buds can float up and down the cup for three times.
- Junshan Silver Needles is the representative of yellow tea. Originally produced in Junshan Island, in Yueyang city of Hu'nan Province, there is limited annual supply, making it difficult to find authentic Junshan Silver Needle in the market. Most of the Junshan Silver Needles currently found in the market are actually Green Tea Silver Needles. Junshan Silver Needles also known as "gold inlaid jade" are dry, thick strips covered with tiny golden hair. One thousand grams of Junshan Silver Needles is approximately fifty thousand tea bud leaves. Because of its characteristic "three rises and falls" while brewing, Junshan Silver Needles is also known as "Xiaoping Tea" in its area of produce, indicating Deng Xiaoping's ups and downs in his political life.
- If you visit Junshan island, you must definitely try a cup of Junshan Silver Needle tea. The tea is fragrant, clear, bright yellow with a sweet and mellow flavor. If the tea is brewed with the well water from Liu Yi Well, it will taste even more exquisite. To sit by the mist-covered Dongting Lake, and admire the Yueyang Tower from afar while listening to the legends of the queen sisters, Ehuang and Nuying and the love story of Liu Yi and the Little Dragon Lady, it is indeed one of the best experiences of life.

Column 6 

Tea in the Kitchen

You can use tea leaves to offer a drink to your guests and also as food. Tea leaves make delicious dishes.

Innovative Uses of Tea Leaves in the Kitchen

While stewing beef, add one or two bags of black tea along with the flavoring. The beef will cook faster and taste better. If a pot or pan retains the smell after being used to cook seafood, boil a few tea leaves in the pot or wipe it with used tea leaves. You will find the smell gone before you know it. Wiping kitchen utensils with used tea leaves is also effective in removing oil and dirt.

Adding Tea Leaves in Dishes

Using tea leaves in food is not a new idea. Even today, people of the Kinuo tribe in Yunnan use tea leaves in their salad. Even tea restaurants and banquet halls use tea leaves in recipes.

Tea Entrees

Tea leaves not only can be used to cook tea eggs, they can also be used to cook noodles or porridge.

Long Jing Prawns Recipe

Ingredients:

400g of peeled prawns, 3-5g Long Jing tea leaves, half egg white, starch, salt, oil.

Method:

Boil the tea leaves and separate the tea leaves and tea liquid.

Clean the prawns, place them in a container and marinate with salt, egg white and starch for 15 minutes.

Fry the prawns and pass it through cold water to remove the oil before returning it into the frying pan. Add the Long Jing tea leaves and stir fry. Add a small amount of tea liquid before serving.

- Replace the Long Jing tea with Bi Luo Chun, Taiping Houkui, Liu'an Guapian or other types of tea for different flavors.
- Use tea liquid instead of cornstarch.

Oolong Tea Rice

After brewing Tieguanyin in a big teapot, pour the tea liquid into the rice cooker and add washed rice. Add water to the amount used to cook rice and begin steaming. Alternatively, one can choose to moisturize the tea leaves before adding it directly into the rice cooker to cook with the rice.

Black Tea Porridge

Boil water on high heat. Add rice with one or two bags of black tea. When the rice is almost cooked, remove the tea bags and simmer the rice. In summer, add black tea ice cubes in the cooked porridge and stir gently.

Tea Dumplings and Noodles

When making the dough for noodles, add a small amount of green tea power (5g for 2–3 servings). Alternatively use tea liquid and noodles.

★ Tea Tips ★

- When cooking tea rice, do not add too much tea leaves. 8–10g is usually enough for 2–3 servings. When the rice is cooked, the tea leaves will float to the top.
- Use any type of tea as per preference.
- Mirco tea powder refers to tea powder of 200 meshes and above, it is also known as matcha powder. It can be added directly to the dishes and is used in many other ways.

Ethereal White Tea

White tea is a special tea product of China. It is lightly fermented. It is mainly produced in Fuding, Zhenghe, Songxi and Jianyang areas of Fujian Province. Available species include Baihao Silver Needles, White Peony, Gongmei, Shoumei, etc. It is usually exported overseas to places having considerable Chinese population, such as Australia, Hongkong and Southeast Asia.

Basic White Tea Knowledge

Water temperature	Approximately 80°
Ratio of tea leaves to water	1:50
Appropriate tea sets	Includes glass and porcelain teacup (teapot)

White Tea Facts

- The method of brewing white tea is similar to that of green tea.
- "Anji White Tea" despite its name is not a type of white tea, rather green tea. Anji White Tea lovers should not confuse Anji White Tea with white tea.

Anji White Tea

Blooms of Water:
White Peony

Pre-brewing Preparation

- Preparing the tea set: Kettle, tea towel, tea coaster, small porcelain cup, teaspoon, tea plate, basin and tea tray.
- Pour the necessary amount of water into the kettle and bring to boil. Let the temperature drop to 80° before use.
- Gently scoop the White Peony Tea leaves onto the tea plate.

Brewing

1 Tea set

↑ Arrange the tea set for brewing.

2 Warming the cup

↑ Pour a small amount of heated water into the cup.

3 Adding tea leaves

↑ Gently add the White Peony Tea leaves into the cup.

4 Moisturizing tea leaves

↑ Pour a small amount of heated water to moisturize the leaves for 10 seconds.

5 Formal brewing

↑ Pour heated water from a height into the cup until 7/10 full.

Offering tea

↑ Offer the freshly brewed tea to the guests with both hands.

More White Tea Information

- White tea is sweet in taste. It is cooling and relaxing and soothes the body and relieves inflammation.
- When brewing top-grade white tea—Baihao Silver Needles—it is best to use a glass teacup. The method of brewing is similar to that of Junshan Silver Needles.
- White tea is not rolled and shaped during processing. It needs about 5 minutes of steeping.
- The floral-shaped White Peony Tea is bright yellow in color. It is sweet and refreshing.

Column 7

Finding a Home for Tea

Tea leaves need to be stored carefully to preserve their quality. Untended leaves grow moldy leading to wastage.

Why Do Tea Leaves Spoil?

Over time tea leaves undergo change. They wither, the color darkens, the flavor ages and the fragrance fades. Sometimes, they even absorb odd scents and mold. This affects the taste. To store tea leaves, take the following four conditions into consideration:

Temperature: The higher the temperature, the faster the change. Store in a place with temperature below 4°.

Humidity: Tea leaves absorb moisture quickly. The water content of tea leaves is usually not higher than 6%, so the higher the humidity, the higher the possibility of the leaves turning wet and soggy.

Oxygen: The oxygen in the air is usually around 20%. The polyphenol and vitamins in the leaves oxidize when they come in contact with air.

Light: If the tea leaves are kept in a transparent container or bag and frequently exposed to the light, the tea leaves will darken and the fragrance will change.

Common Storage Methods

Freezer

Seal the tea leaves in a bag and deep freeze. Take care not to keep it next to items with strong scents. In case of large amount of tea leaves, store in an individual freezer. The temperature should be kept at 3° to 5°.

Quick lime

Choose an airtight container such as a clay jar. Seal quick lime inside a cotton bag and place it inside the container. Wrap the tea leaves properly with cotton paper and place it on top of the quick lime bag. Seal the container and place it in a cool, dry, unscented place.

Vacuum packaging

Place the tea leaves in a ziplock bag and extract all the air. Seal the bag inside a container and store it in a cool dry place. This method is suitable for storing grain-shaped Oolong tea. However, the tea leaves are easily crushed when extracting air. Ask for the tea leaves to be vacuumed packaged when buying tea leaves.

Choosing Storage Containers

Tea leaves are usually stored in paper, wood, porcelain or tin containers. Choose an unscented and airtight container. Different tea leaves should be stored in different containers. Do not use the same container to store different type of tea leaves. Do not use a container previously used to store a different type of tea for storing another type of leaves. This is especially important for containers used to store floral tea leaves. Do not directly store tea leaves in containers, rather keep in ziplock bags before keeping in the container.

In conclusion, keep in mind that tea leaves should be stored in cool, dry, dark places. Keep away from oxygen and strong fragrances. If you take note of all these conditions when storing tea leaves, the tea leaves should keep for a long time.

More Tips

- Top-quality green tea leaves and lightly fermented Oolong tea leaves must be sealed and kept in the freezer.
- Floral teas must be sealed individually to prevent absorption of other fragrances.
- When storing Pu-erh tea leaves, remember to remove its packaging and store naturally in a clay jar in a cool, dry, dark and unscented place.
- After taking out the tea leaves, remember to replace it in its original spot. The teaspoon used must be dry. Do not take more than necessary as unused tea leaves, exposed in the air for a long time, should not be returned to the tea jar.

A Bouquet of Floral Tea

Floral Tea Production Process

Raw tea and fresh flowers

↓

Mixing tea and flowers

↓

Fumigation

↓

Drying

Basic Floral Tea Knowledge

Water temperature	Water temperature depends on the type of tea used as the raw tea. If the raw tea is made from green tea, such as Jasmine Silver Needles, maintain the water temperature at approximately 85°. If the raw tea is made from black tea, such as Rose Black Tea, the water temperature must be above 95°. If the raw tea is made from Oolong tea, such as Osmanthus Oolong Tea, then the water should be at boiling point.
Amount of tea leaves	The ratio of leaves to water should be 1:50
Appropriate tea sets	Include tea bowl or porcelain teacup with lids, or teapots

Floral Tea Facts

Floral tea is reprocessed tea. It is made by mixing tea leaves and fragrant flowers and allowing tea leaves to absorb the fragrance of the flowers.

Renowned Fragrance:
Jasmine Tea

Pre-brewing Preparation

- Preparation of the tea set: Kettle, tea bowl, basin, tea plate, teaspoon and tea towel.
- Pour the necessary amount of water into the kettle and bring to boil. Allow the water temperature to drop to 85° before use.
- Scoop the necessary amount of jasmine tea leaves into the tea plate.

Brewing

1 Tea set

→ Arrange the tea set for brewing.

2 Warming the tea bowl

↑ Pour the heated water into the tea bowl.

↑ Cover with the lid and rotate the tea bowl.

3 Adding tea leaves

↑ Add the jasmine tea leaves into the tea bowl.

4 Adding water

↑ Fill the tea bowl with heated water until 7/10 full and cover the tea bowl properly.

Offering tea

↑ Offer the freshly brewed tea to the guests with both hands.

Appreciating the fragrance

↑ Hold the tea saucer with one hand and tilt the cover with the other to gently breathe in the fragrance.

Appreciating the tea

↑ Before drinking, gently use the lid of the tea bowl to brush across the surface of the tea to sweep away the tea leaves.

↑ Tilt the lid of the tea bowl and breathe in the fragrance and sip the tea through the opening gap.

More Jasmine Tea Information

- When brewing jasmine tea, you may occasionally, catch the fragrance of the white flowers. This is because when fumigating jasmine tea, usually a small amount of magnolias is used for a base.
- Jasmine tea leaves must be stored carefully.

Creativity in Tea: Ornamental Floral Tea

Ornamental Floral Tea is made by tying flowers and tea leaves together in a floral design. Upon brewing, the design absorbs water and expands into a pretty floral arrangement floating in the tea.

Basic Ornamental Floral Tea Knowledge

Requirement	One bundle of floral tea leaves is added per teacup/teapot
Water temperature	90° and above
Capacity	The teapot or teacup should be big, with a capacity above 200ml
Appropriate tea sets	Include glass teapot or teacups that can withstand high temperature

Ornamental Floral Tea Facts

- When adding water while brewing ornamental floral tea, avoid pouring directly on to the tea leaves or the floral design might disintegrate.
- The main focus of ornamental floral tea is in its design, the taste is secondary.
- Ornamental floral tea takes a few minutes to expand to its intended shape. Sometimes, the design may face down. Adjust with the tea pick.

Various Ornamental Floral Tea Designs

Seven Fairies

↑Tea leaves →

↑Adding water →

↑Blooming in the water

Marigolds

↑Tea leaves →

↑Adding water →

↑Blooming in the water

Lotus Lantern

↑Tea leaves →

↑Adding water →

↑Blooming in the water

Water Lilies

↑ Tea leaves →

↑ Adding water →

↑ Blooming in the water

Red Osmanthus

↑ Tea leaves →

↑ Adding water →

↑ Blooming in the water

Golden Gourd

↑ Tea leaves →

↑ Adding water →

↑ Blooming in the water

Column 8

Floral and Herbal Tea

We drink herbal tea for many reasons, but most importantly to balance the body and relax. The rippling colors of the blooming flowers and herbs in the water greatly aid in meditating and relaxing both body and mind.

Herbs and Flowers of Various Shapes and Colors

Golden Lotus Tea

↑The golden lotus is gold in color and refreshing in taste. It aids in clearing and soothing the throat and relieving inflammation. Use 1 to 2 buds per cup.

Jade Butterfly Tea

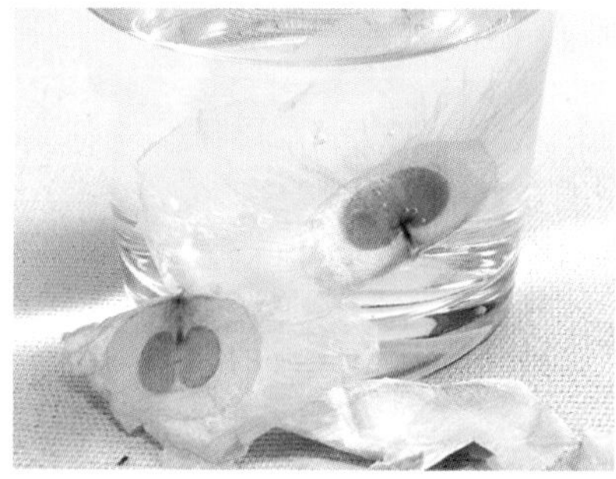

↑ The jade butterfly is crystal clear in color. It aids in soothing the throat. Use 3 to 4 slices per cup. The jade butterfly is the seed of the Jade Butterfly plant and is not a type of flower.

Bamboo Leaf Tea

↑ The bamboo leaf tea is light green in color and slightly bitter to taste. It aids in clearing the mind and cooling the body. Use 1 to 2g per cup.

Forget-me-not Tea

↑ Forget-me-not is light in taste and aids in cooling the body and clearing the lungs. Use 5 to 7 buds per cup. Forget-me-not is both yellow and purple.

Gomphrena Tea

↑ Gomphrena tea is light and ethereal. It aids in cleansing the liver and easing breathing. Use 2 to 3 buds per cup.

Gold Chrysanthemum

↑ Gold chrysanthemum cools the body, relieves inflammation and brightens the eyes. Use 3 to 5 buds per cup. The petals will unfurl upon absorbing water, resembling a freshly picked chrysanthemum.

Jasmine Tea

↑ Jasmine tea has a delicate and ethereal fragrance, and can be used to soothe frazzled nerves and refresh the mind. Use approximately 10 buds per cup.

Lavender Tea

↑ Lavender tea is slightly bitter in taste. It can be used to soothe frazzled nerves and is a good for aiding sleep. Use approximately 1g per cup.

Column 8

Rose Tea

↑ Rose tea has a slightly bitter taste. It is good for regulating blood circulation and skin clarification. Therefore it is a favorite among ladies. Use 6 to 8 buds per cup.

Azalea Tea

↑ Azalea tea has a light fragrance and a slightly bitter taste. It is good for regulating blood circulation and skin clarification. Use 4 to 5 petals per cup.

Brewing Herbal Tea

- Choose glass teapots and teacups that can withstand high temperature. Prepare the herbs on a tea plate and bring the water to boil.
- First pour some heated water into the teapot to warm the teapot and teacup.
- Use a teaspoon to add the herbs into the teapot or teacup. Place the herbs in the strainer or infuser.
- Add water, wait for a few minutes and the tea will be ready.

Brewing Techniques

- Usually transparent glass teapot or teacup is used to brew herbal or floral tea to admire the flowers or herbs unfurling slowly as it absorbs the water. Some tea liquid will even change color. If the herbs used are small, such as lavender, brew them with an infuser or strainer.

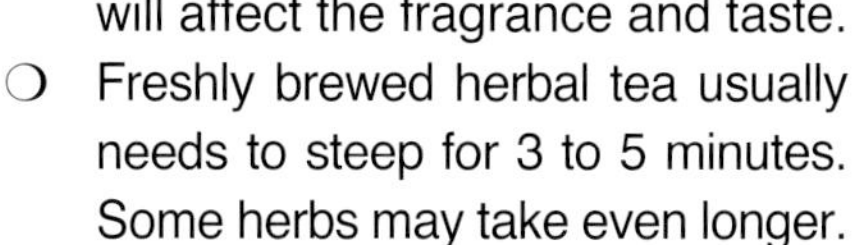

- Herbal tea should be brewed in boiling water. If the water temperature isn't high enough, it will affect the fragrance and taste.
- Freshly brewed herbal tea usually needs to steep for 3 to 5 minutes. Some herbs may take even longer.

★ Tea Tips ★
When brewing small, broken herbs, in the absence of a strainer, put in a tea bag before putting it in the cup.

- You can drink herbal tea just as it is or with sugar or honey. You can brew it with other types of tea leaves or herbs. Dried herbs can also be brewed with fresh herbs.
- You can brew good herbal tea leaves for a number of rounds.

Storing Herbal Tea Leaves

Store herbal tea leaves in a cool dry place. Seal properly to keep dry. If used infrequently, store in the freezer. It can usually keep for 1 to 2 years. Herbal tea leaves are susceptible to breeding small worms. However, as long as it is sealed tightly in a freezer, there is no need to worry.

Part 3

Origins of Tea

China is the birthplace of tea. During the Tang and Song dynasties, the Chinese drank compressed tea. It was during the Ming and Qing dynasties that the people slowly turned to drinking loose tea. Brewing tea methods also changed from roasting and tencha to the current methods of brewing tea.

Pre-Sui and Tang Dynasty Tea Customs

China first discovered, grew and used tea leaves. The growth of tea and the related customs in other countries came directly or indirectly from China. Even the pronunciation of the word "tea" originated from Chinese dialects.

Shennong and the Tea Antidote

The legendary Yan emperor Shennong was known as the pioneer of agriculture. According to legends, one day, Shennong accidentally ate a poisonous herb and immediately felt faint. He dragged himself to the nearest tree. He swallowed the bittersweet leaves and immediately felt better. He recovered soon after. That antidote was what we call tea today. It is not important if Shennong was only a legend. The important point is that even 5,000 years ago, the Chinese used tea leaves. In the beginning, they picked the fresh tea leaves. However, as fresh tea leaves were not suitable for storing or shipping, they slowly began drying and storing tea leaves.

Tea as a drink

The transition of tea from a medicine and food to a drink is said to have started in the Zhou Dynasty. It is believed that when King Wu attacked King Zhou, Zhou was forced to travel south. Unaccustomed to the climate and food, his soldiers were weakened and fatigued. Prince Zhou ordered his serfs to cook tea leaves in huge pots. This custom spread. By the time of the Han Dynasty, drinking tea had become a fashionable custom.

The "Pageboy Contract"

During the time of the western Han Dynasty, once the lyricist Wang Bao bought a servant Bian Liao from his friend's widow. Bian Liao was unwilling, but there was nothing he could do. He told Wang Bao, "You must clearly state everything you want me to do in a contract. If it isn't stated in the contract, I won't do it." This became the "Pageboy Contract" that we see today. In the contract, Wang Bao clearly stated "Buying tea in Wuyang" and "Brewing Tea with the tea set."

The contract reveals that even during that time, one had to buy tea from Wuyang (currently the Mt. Peng area in Sichuan), and there were specific tea sets for brewing tea.

Tea drinking further spread toward the mid and lower Yangtze River areas from the Han Dynasty to the time of the Southern and Northern dynasties.

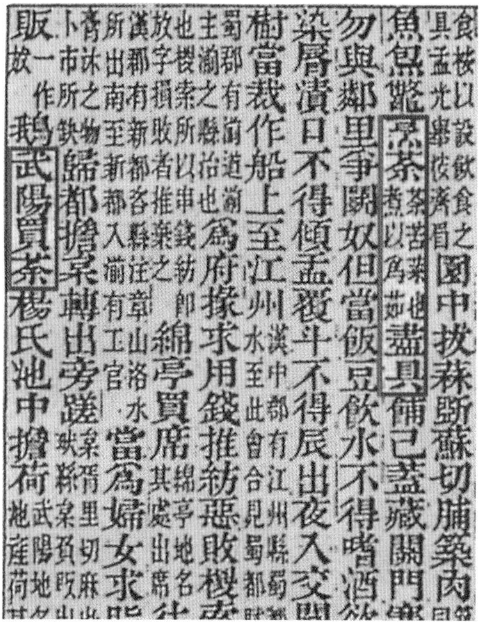

↑ A copy of western Han's "Pageboy Contract".

The Secret Decree

According to the records in the "Biography of Wei Yao" in the volume "History of Wu" in *The History of the Three Kingdoms,* the reigning monarch of the Kingdom of Wu, Sun Hao, was a lover of wine. Wei Yao, a knowledgeable and talented official of his kingdom unfortunately could not hold his drink. To save him from embarrassing himself, Sun Hao secretly changed his wine into a liquid of a similar color, tea. This shows that both tea and wine were beverages that were frequently used in court. Even today, people who cannot hold their alcohol use tea to toast each other.

Tea as a Sign of Honor

Once in the time of the eastern Jin Dynasty, Lu Na, the Minster of Officials entertained prime minister Xie An with fruits and tea. Lu Na's nephew, afraid of offending the prime minister by this meager offering, prepared a table of expensive dishes. Lu Na angrily reprimanded his nephew for being wasteful. His actions had tarnished the honorable and frugal name of his house. Entertaining guests with tea is not miserly, nor is it a sign of arrogance. It is a sign of frugality and honor, and it fits with the pure nature of tea.

Tea as a Burial Item

The large number of items evacuated from Lady Hou, Xin Zhui's tomb, included an entire box of tea leaves. This shows tea used to be part of the burial offerings during the Han Dynasty.

Tea in Ancestral Worship

Emperor Wu of the southern Qi Dynasty, Xiao Yu, was an open-minded and frugal emperor, who cared for the welfare of his people. Before his death, he decreed, "Keep my burial frugal. Just offer fruits and tea. " He also ordered that everyone should follow this custom.

Tea is not only an antidote for poison or thirst; it can replace wine to entertain guests, as a burial item or in ancestral or religious worship. Its uses, both physical and spiritual, are far beyond its natural attributes. The Buddhists loved tea giving it an even richer cultural meaning. At the same time, Confucians and Taoists also integrated tea drinking in their customs. Royals, scholars, Confucians, Taoists and Buddhists supported the drinking of tea.

Sui and Tang Dynasty Tea Customs

Though the Sui Dynasty did not rule for a long time, Emperor Yang built the Grand Canal, making it possible for the southern tea leaves to be shipped to the north. The economic development during the Tang Dynasty led the production and sale of tea leaves to reach unparalleled heights. The distribution center of tea leaves moved to the Jiangzhe area. During this period both tea and the social culture of China developed rapidly.

Lu Yu and the *Classic of Tea*

During the mid-Tang Dynasty, there were numerous tea poems, tea paintings and tea books, the most famous of which was Lu Yu's *Classic of Tea.* The *Classic of Tea* consists of three volumes and ten chapters with approximately seven thousand words. The first chapter is dedicated to the origin of tea—the names of tea and its effects. The second records the equipments used in tea production. The third chapter is on tea production—the suitable time for harvesting tea, ways of harvesting and producing tea, as well as the different varieties and qualities of tea. The fourth chapter is on tea sets in detail. The fifth chapter is on brewing tea. It records methods of baking and roasting tea as well as choosing the most suitable water to brew tea. The sixth chapter is about drinking tea—the history and customs of tea drinking. The seventh chapter talks about the stories of tea and its medicinal virtues. The eighth chapter talks about the famous production areas of tea in the Tang Dynasty. The ninth chapter describes the equipments used in picking, making and drinking tea. It discusses which equipments are necessary and which are unnecessary. The tenth chapter is a painting of the content of the *Classic of Tea* on a silk cloth that can be hung in the living room for easy reference. The *Classic of Tea* is the first book on tea in the world and has a deep influence on the future tea culture.

↑ A copy of Tang Dynasty's *Classic of Tea.*

Lu Yu Roasting Tea

The Tang Dynasty usually brewed tea from steamed Oolong tea disks. They focused on the technique of roasting tea. Lu Yu, the Tea Sage, was a master in roasting tea. It was said that during the time of Daizong Emperor, Reverend Zhiji of Longgai Tempel in Jingling (today's Tianmen city of Hubei) was once invited to the palace. The emperor ordered his best tea roaster to roast the best quality tea for the reverend. After the first sip, the reverend set down his tea bowl and did not take another sip. When asked, the reverend answered, "I only drink tea that is roasted by my disciple, Lu Yu. Other teas taste bland to me." The emperor wanted to meet Lu Yu. Zhiji said, "He is away searching for the best teas and best waters in the world." So, the emperor sent people to search for Lu Yu. When he finally met him, the emperor ordered him to roast a cup of tea for him. Lu Yu roasted a cup of tea and offered it to the emperor. The tea was clear and light green with a delicate fragrance. He took a sip, and the sweetness of the tea filled his mouth. He nodded his head in approval. He agreed only Lu Yu could roast such good tea.

↑ Tang Dynasty *Palace Joy*.

Method of Roasting Tea

Tea Roasting is also known as Tea Cooking. The tea used in roasting is a steamed Oolong tea disk. Hold the tea disk by a pair of bamboo tongs and bake above a fire to remove the moisture, making it easier to grind. Bake the tea disk over medium fire, rotating frequently. If the tea leaves were baked dry, bake until it is no longer steaming. If it was sun-dried, bake until tender. After baking, place the tea in a paper bag immediately to avoid moisture. After it is cooled, grind it into granular tea dust. Do not grind into powder. Brush the tea dust into the pan. Cover the pan and shake it lightly. Heat the water over charcoal first before roasting the tea. Do not use fuel that will produce scent or smoke. The quality of the water is very important in roasting tea. Spring water is the best. River water second and well water is the worst. Pour the water into the pot and begin boiling. Small bubbles begin to appear and you can hear light bubbling sounds. This is known as the "first boil." Spoon a little salt into the tea. When the water bubbles continuously, it is known as the "second boil." Scoop a ladle of the heated water aside and use a pair of bamboo chopsticks to stir the water. Use the tea scoop to add the tea dust into the whirlpool and continue cooking. The water from the "second boil" is just right for roasting tea.

Let the tea in the pot continue to boil and bubble. This is known as the "third boil." Pour the ladle of water from the second boil into the tea and you will see the essence of the tea—steamed foam and froth. Place the pot on the coaster and ladle the tea into the bowls. Distribute the foam evenly. Lu Yu believed only the water from the second boil gives the perfect taste of roasted tea. Thick steam, thin foam and light froth are the essence of the tea. Usually, the first three bowls of the tea taste better than the last two. The taste of a good roasted tea is bitter at the first sip and sweet when swallowed.

Due to Lu Yu's efforts, roasted tea became very popular. Steamed Oolong tea was also made into loose tea leaves, coarse tea leaves and powdered tea leaves. Apart from adding salt, some people added garlic, ginger, dates, orange peels or peppermint.

10 virtues of tea drinking

To dispel depression, to dispel sleepiness, to increase vitality, to dispel illnesses, to encourage compassion, to show respect, to taste flavors, to improve health, tea can touch the heart, tea can uphold morals – Tang, Liu Zhenliang.

Toward the end of the Tang Dynasty and early Song Dynasty, the technique of tea production improved. The way of drinking tea turned from roasting to whisking, also known as tencha.

Song and Yuan Dynasties Tea Customs

During the Song Dynasty, the production scale expanded greatly. The technique of tea production became even more refined. The famous Dragon and Phoenix tea disk was produced at that time. It was also known as Piancha. During production, the mold used to make the tea disk was engraved with a dragon and phoenix design. The court specially sent officials to monitor the process of tribute tea production. Dragon and Phoenix tea was originally 500g per 8 disks. Later, it became 500g per 20 disks.

Zhao Ji and *Da Guan Theories of Tea*

All the emperors of the Song Dynasty were tea lovers. They frequently held tea gatherings in the palace. Emperor Huizong, Zhao Ji was the author of the book, *Da Guan Theories of Tea.* He was the first emperor in history to write a book on tea. Huizong was a master in the art of tea, and frequently personally brewed tencha for his officials. *Da Guan Theories of Tea* has 20 chapters. It records in detail the production place, the environment, the climate, the time and method of harvest, the process of steaming and producing tea, the methods of distinguishing the quality of tea disks, the various equipment and water used in tencha. It also records the color, fragrance and taste of various tea leaves, the baking and storing of tea leaves, the names of tea leaves, etc.

↑ Song Dynasty *Da Guan Theories of Tea.*

Tencha Technique

Tencha brewing was very common in the Song Dynasty. The popular brewing method was usually tencha. The Japanese monks who came to China to study during the Song Dynasty took back to Japan the tencha brewing method, still in use today. The Japanese art of matcha was born from the Song Dynasty's tencha. Tencha is directly brewed in heated water and not simmered or cooked over charcoal fire. One method is to whisk directly in the teacup. The other method is to whisk the tea in the tea bowl before ladling the tea into the individual cups.

When brewing tencha, one must first bake the tea disk. If the disc has been produced in the current year, grind immediately after baking. If it is an aged tea disc, first soak in boiling water. Scrape off one or two layers of the oil on the surface before picking it with tea tongs and baking it over a low fire to remove the aged scent. Wrap in paper and beat it before grinding it into powder form. Then pass through a sieve to ensure that the tea is as fine as possible.

Next, boil water. The water must be light, clear, sweet and from a running source. Before brewing tencha, listen for the first boil, the second boil and the third boil... The water temperature after the third boil is most suitable because it is the temperature where the tea is most soluble. Warm the teacup before adding the tea. Add the sieved tea powder, and add a small amount of water. Make a paste before adding heated water. Whisk the mixture repeatedly until froth appears. The tea liquid should be pure white.

Another method is whisking the tea in a tea bowl. When whisking, use a light the hand to whisk strongly. In the first round of water, add only a small amount. Swirl the water into the cup and do not pour directly. Make a paste. In the second round, directly pour the water. In the third round, pour the water while whisking, so that it froths at the surface. In the fourth round, add a little water. In the fifth round, the amount of water depends on the amount of froth. In the sixth round, add the water while slowly stirring the tea with the whisk. In the seventh round, the tencha is completed. Distribute the tea into the teacups evenly so that each cup has a balanced amount of froth. Do not add salt as the tea should maintain its original flavor.

↑ Song Dynasty, *Grinding Tea Leaves*, partial.

Tea Competition

Tea competition is the ability to distinguish the quality of the tea. It began in the Tang Dynasty and became a social game of comparing tea quality and competing tea techniques. In a tea competition, the first item on the agenda is the quality of tea disks. The tea disks must be made from tender fresh leaves and finely produced. The quality of the tea disks directly affect the color of the tea liquid. The liquid should be pure white. In order to protect the tea disk from absorbing other scents or dampness, a layer of oil is applied to the surface and it is wrapped in bamboo paper before being put in a tea basket.

Next is the tencha technique. This includes the choosing and boiling of water. Spring water is the best. The most difficult part of boiling the water is distinguishing the temperature through listening to the sound of boiling water. Alternatively, the quality of the tea leaves can also be used to determine the temperature of the water. Tender tea leaves are brewed with young water. The froth on the tea is also an important factor. It should be pure white in color, lasting, slender and balanced. The longer the liquid is hidden under the froth, the better the quality of the tea. The finer the tea, the easier it is for the tea to dissolve in the water and form froth. In order to highlight the pure white color of the tea, use a black teacup. The teacup should be deep and with a large width. The best teacup is the rabbit-hair teacup from Jian'an kiln of that era. The cup is heavy and keeps the tea warm. In addition, when whisking the tea, use a strong whisk or teaspoon. Use a small kettle to boil the water. The spout should be long with a tiny mouth. This makes it easier to tell the temperature.

↑ Yuan Dynasty, *Tea Competition Scene.*

"Fen Cha," Tea Art

"Fen Cha" is also known as the "theater of tea." It is a game that began among the people of the northern Song Dynasty. In this, one has to first grind the tea into powder, then pour it into the teacup. Next, add water, whisk and form an image on the surface of the liquid. This is known as "water calligraphy." It is said that a master tea artist, a monk named Fuquan, could whisk four cups of tea at the same time and produce tea with images of poetry, landscape paintings, floral and animal paintings. Sadly, this art has long since been lost.

The culture of drinking tea began in the Tang Dynasty and gained popularity in the Song Dynasty. This reflects the prosperity of that era. Tea is not merely an important item of life. The emperors' love for tea resulted in the inclusion of tea in court. The scholars' love of tea resulted in a legacy of many tea poems, tea paintings and tea books. Teahouses filled the streets, providing entertainment venues for the people. Many tea-related customs were created as well.

Steamed Oolong loose leaf tea was sold in the market, and became an alternative simpler way of brewing tea. Tea disks were replaced by loose leaf tea.

Ming and Qing Tea Customs

During the Ming and Qing dynasties, tea production improved greatly. In 1381, the first emperor of the Ming Dynasty, Zhu Yuanzhang promoted the development of loose tea leaves. The production of green tea developed from steamed green tea to pan-dried green tea. Other tea varieties, such as floral tea, dark tea, black tea, Oolong tea, white tea and yellow tea also made their appearance. Tea drinking became a simple process of adding tea leaves in a tea bowl or teapot and adding heated water. This method retained the original flavor and scent of the tea leaves.

Zhang Yuan and the Tea Records

Ming Dynasty published the most number of tea books in China. The most famous and representative of these tea books is Zhang Yuan's *Tea Records.* The book contains more than 1,500 words. The content touched on picking tea, distinguishing tea, storing tea, identifying the temperature of the water, methods of brewing, methods of adding tea leaves, the color, fragrance and taste of tea, choosing quality spring or well water, storing water, tea sets, etc. It is notable for proposing new views on brewing tea. Zhang Yuan believed that dried green tea should be boiled with boiling water in order to achieve the true flavor of the tea. He also proposed that the teapot should be warmed before adding tea leaves. He was very particular about adding tea leaves. Zhang Yuan also proposed that when appreciating tea, the less the number of people present the better. The spirit of tea is best appreciated alone. These were all ideas not previously seen in the *Classic of Tea.*

Kangxi and Qianlong (Qing Dynasty) left behind many tea poems. Qianlong alone wrote more than 200 tea poems. In addition, he left 18 royally planted tea plants. He also named Beijing's Jade Springs as the top spring of the world.

Gongfu Tea

According to research, Gongfu tea originated in the later Ming Dynasty. It gained popularity in the Qing Dynasty and was renowned in Chaozhou. Gongfu tea was produced in Fujian Province. Today, almost every household in Chaozhou has a Gongfu tea set. To brew a cup of Gongfu tea during family reunions or when friends come to visit is a Chaozhou and Guangdong custom. Gongfu Teas was originally the name of a type of tea leaf. It refers to the best quality Wuyi Yan tea leaf. During the reign of Emperor Yongzheng of the Qing Dynasty, Lu Yancan, governor of Cong'an Prefecture in Fujian (the current Wuyi Shan City) once quoted the following passage from *Observation Records* in his book, *Sequel to the Classic of Tea,* "In Mt Wuyi, tea leaves picked from the top of the mountain is known as Yan Tea. Tea leaves picked from the waterside is known as Zhou Tea. Yan Tea is top quality, Zhou Tea is second. Yan Tea from the northern peak is the best; Yan Tea from the southern peak is second. The two types of tea leaves are named after the mountains from where they were picked. The best of these are known as 'Gongfu Tea.'"

↑ Ming Dynasty, *Huishan Tea Gathering,* partial image.

The earliest recorded method of brewing Gongfu tea is in the 51st year of the reign of Qianlong Emperor of the Qing Dynasty. It was recorded by Yuan Mei (1716–1797) in his book, *Sui Yuan Recipes.* In the chapter "Wine and Tea," under Wuyi Tea, he recorded, "The cup should be as small as a walnut, the pot as small as a citron. Each brew will not exceed 50 gram. One would not bear to sip it immediately, but will first inhale its scent before taking a sip. One would slowly sip the brew and appreciate the taste..." The text records in detail his travels in Mt. Wuyi. Everyone offered their guests tea brewed in a small teapot and drank from tiny cups. He also recorded that the custom was to first inhale the scent before taking a sip and that the tea still had a strong flavor even after being brewed for three rounds. These descriptions described using the Gongfu tea brewing method to brew Wuyi tea leaves. Thus, we can see that during mid-Qing Dynasty, Gongfu tea was already popular in the northern Min area.

The formal naming as "Gongfu Tea" was by the Xingning Prefecture's historian Yu Jiao in Guangdong. He detailed the entire process of Gongfu tea brewing method in his book *Mengchang Zazhu*:

- Prepare a stove, a teapot and a tray. Use Zisha teapot and small porcelain teacups. The number of cups depends on the number of guests.
- Use spring water to brew the tea.
- Use charcoal to boil the water, and brew the tea with water that has just reached boiling point.
- Seal the teapot when brewing the tea.
- Sip the tea slowly.

Similar to the methods of brewing tea, the tea set used in the Tang and Song dynasties are very different from that used in the Ming and Qing dynasties. It is said that Su Shi of the Song Dynasty made his own overhead handle Zisha teapot, and that there are numerous famous makers of Zisha teapot in the Ming Dynasty. This particular type of teapot is exceedingly important in the brewing of Gongfu tea.

The brewing of Gongfu tea began and was perfected in the Ming and Qing dynasties. It was popularized in the Min and Yue area, and became the famous Chaoshan Gongfu Tea. It formed the foundation for the modern method of brewing tea and is still one of the most important methods of brewing tea today.

↑ Ming Dynasty, *Lin Xie Roasting Tea*, partial image.

Modern Tea Customs

Different tea leaves require different brewing methods. Modern tea brewers are continuously testing and discovering new brewing methods or changing and perfecting old brewing methods. Gongfu tea, as a type of brewing method, is internationally popular. There are many different schools of Gongfu tea, such as Southern Min Gongfu tea, Taiwan Gongfu tea, Beijing Gongfu tea, Shanghai Gongfu tea, etc. Oolong tea, black tea, dark tea, green tea, yellow tea, white tea, all the teas of the tea family can be brewed in the Gongfu tea brewing method. The tea sets used for Gongfu tea is even more varied. For the teapot, one can use Zisha, porcelain, glass, etc. The tea tray is no longer just a simple round porcelain tray. It now comes in wood, bamboo, stainless steel, clay or stone. It can be double-layered or single-layered. Also, there are additional items such as the fairness cup, aroma cup and the strainer.

Today, the pace of life is fast. Therefore, there are now types of tea that are both fast and convenient. Examples include teabags, instant tea, tea concentrate and even canned or bottled tea. The 21st century is a century of tea. Chinese tea will continue to spread its fragrance and become a universal health drink.

Innovative Uses of Tea in Everyday Lives

Other than as a form of drink or food, tea also plays an important role in health improvement.

- Drinking tea aids in resisting radioactive rays.
- Rinsing the mouth with tea helps prevent tooth decay.
- After eating pungent foods such as ginger or garlic, chewing dry tea leaves will help freshen the mouth.
- If the refrigerator has a lingering odor after long use, placing a plate of tea leaves to make it odorless.
- After house renovation, placing a plate of tea leaves in the house will remove unpleasant scents.

- Bathing with tea liquid clarifies the skin and makes it fragrant. Washing hair in tea liquid leaves the hair silky. Using tea dregs to soak the feet will prevent athlete's feet.
- The mix of egg white and micro green tea powder is an effective facial mask that will clarify and whiten the skin.
- Placing used tea leaves in a gauze bag on the eyes for 15 to 20 minutes will relieve eye fatigue and help reduce dark circles and eye bags.
- Placing used dry leaves in shoes and unused clothes will remove unpleasant odors. They also make good fillings for pillows.
- Burning dried used tea leaves is also a good air freshener and insect repellent.
- After eating meat or oily food, drinking a cup of tea aids digestion.
- When smoking, polyphenols in tea aid in lessening the harmful effects of the toxic compounds in the tobacco.

Bibliography

1. Luan Haogeng. *The Four Types of Earliest Tea.* Hangzhou: Zhejiang Sheying Chubanshe, 2001.
2. Zhou Hongjie. *Yunnan Pu-erh Tea.* Kunming: Yunnan Keji Chubanshe, 2004.
3. Qiu Jiping. *Song Tea Pictorial Records.* Hangzhou: Zhejiang Sheying Chubanshe, 2004.
4. Yu Guanting. *Discussions on Tea Culture.* Beijing: Zhongguo Nongye Chubanshe, 2003.
5. Dong Shangsheng, Wang Jianrong. *History of Tea.* Hangzhou: Zhejiang Daxue Chubanshe, 2003.
6. Chen Qikun, Yang Zhaoli, Yao Guokun. *Lu Yu's Classic of Tea, Intepretation and Annotation.* Shanghai: Shanghai Wenhua Chubanshe, 2003.
7. Chen Xiangbai. *China Tea Culture.* Taiyuan: Shanxi Renmin Chubanshe, 2002.
8. Chen Wenhua. *Basic Knowledge of China Tea Culture.* Beijing: Zhongguo Nongye Chubanshe, 2003.